Ready For Anything

A guide to predator hunting

Written by Glen "rizzo" Stilson

With stories by Scott Francom and Jason LeMarr

Text © 2009 Glen Stilson
Photographs © 2009 Glen Stilson

All rights reserved. No part of this book may be reproduced by any means whatsoever without written permission from the author, except brief portions quoted for the purpose of review.

Published through CreateSpace.com
Order additional copies at:
https://www.createspace.com/3394954

This book was printed in the United States of America

ISBN 1448672775
EAN-13 978-1448672776

Contents

Introduction To Calling — Page 7

Scouting Your Location — Page 13

The Gear — Page 19

Accuracy Counts — Page 37

Stand Selection — Page 44

Call Sequence — Page 52

Animal Behavior — Page 64

Seasons — Page 74

After The Shot — Page 82

Competitions — Page 92

Where's Rizzo? — Page 98

The Future Of Our Sport — Page 116

Closing Advice — Page 123

Other Methods Of Take — Page 125

Product Recommendations — Page 132

About The Author — Page 136

For all the men and women who keep this sport alive . . . . there's always time for one more stand.

The sun was still below the horizon as I made my way to the stand location I had scouted out the week before. I knew there were coyotes in the area, as I had seen many of them while hunting for rabbits. The early morning October air held a chill as I climbed the hillside, picking my way through the maze of prickly pear cacti on the ground. As I neared the location from which I would call, I heard the distinct barking and yipping of coyotes, but they were far off in the distance. Even still, my heart began to beat faster and I felt as though I could hear the blood rushing through my body – I was about to hunt a predator. As the sun began to crest the horizon, I chose a spot under a large juniper tree and sat down, my back to the rising sun and a gentle breeze blowing across my face. I rested my rifle in front of me on its bipod, pulled the face mask up over my face, and put my "Tally-Ho" call to my mouth. I started to send the sounds of a distressed and dying rabbit across the plains, through the valleys and washes, and into the underbrush where the animals make their homes. As I continued to blow the call, I began to inflect more emotion into the sound, as if I were a rabbit pleading with some unknown force to save me from this fate. I allowed a pause to fill the air as I scanned the valley below and the hill on which I sat for any signs of movement, but there was none. I resumed my screaming as I envisioned hordes of coyotes descending upon my location, all fighting for the chance to devour their would-be meal. After a few more minutes of calling, I paused again, watching and listening as if I could somehow hear the cautious predator approaching. I started my third set of death cries, blowing as persuasively as I could into the call, when suddenly I caught movement from the corner of my right eye. I turned my head to see a coyote, in the flesh, standing no more than 15 yards from me, looking quickly and expertly for the source of the noise. Our eyes met as I swung my rifle towards him. He turned to run just as my finger found the breaking point of the trigger, sending forth lead and copper to put him down for good. I could barely believe my eyes as there before me lay my first called coyote. The action has not stopped since.

Introduction To Calling

Predator calling has grown in popularity in leaps and bounds over the past few years. A sport that once drew only a certain type of sportsman is now enjoyed by all types of hunters, from the seasonal deer hunter to upland bird pursuers. And once you get the bug, once you've seen that coyote or fox or bobcat approaching you, headed straight for your stand, it's not hard to understand why so many people enjoy it.

My first bobcat, a big 30 pound female

Predator hunting began for me while I was pursuing other game animals. Growing up, I would head to the deserts of Arizona with my friends to hunt rabbits and shoot the occasional coyote. Soon the rabbits began to lose their appeal and it was just the coyotes that I wanted. I used the Johnny Stewart tapes and the old green Circe calls, and was doing everything I could to entice the coyotes I saw to come a little closer. But something in my method was lacking. Then I watched a predator hunting video and understood what I was missing – stealth and surprise! So I took a couple hand calls, got into some camo, snuck into a stand and 20 minutes into my first set I had killed my first coyote. I came back the next day and not 50 yards away I called another one in and killed it. My first two stands and two coyotes dead and I was hooked for life.

When I discuss predator hunting with people, many cannot understand why I would want to kill these beautiful animals. Truth be told, I don't keep many coyote pelts, and while I keep all of my bobcat and fox pelts, they're more for my collection or bartering than to sell. So why do I kill them? I'm not a fan of stats, so I won't quote any here. However, if you start researching the effects of predator hunting on local big game populations, you'll find that hunters are once again to thank for keeping elk, deer, and antelope herd numbers stabilized and populations healthy. In many places where I hunt, the predator to prey ratio is too high and as stewards of the land it is up to us to maintain healthy numbers of all animals, which means we need to take down some predators. I also hunt on a lot of ranches where the local predator population is damaging to livestock and pet numbers, and it seems that no matter how many I kill, there are just as many the next year. It is also an exciting sport, where you must outsmart the natural hunter. I have had more close encounters and seen more wildlife while calling predators and sitting motionless and camouflaged than I ever saw while creeping through the woods deer hunting.

So now that I've covered why I hunt and how I got into it, let's take a look at how calling predators can be accomplished by anyone willing to take the time and effort to learn how. There are many people who grab a call and some camo and go into the woods hoping to call a predator. After a few minutes or a few stands they give up and decide it's all too boring or that they are simply no good at it. Truth be told, they probably called something in, but without the proper guidance or experience they were not trained to be in the right place to see it.

Garret on one of his first rabbit hunts with me when he was about three-years-old. He came up with the term "Rabbit Eyes".

For most people, seeing animals in the wild is an acquired skill. Anyone can look around and see something sometimes, but to see everything all the time takes practice. My son, Garret, calls this skill "Rabbit Eyes". I take him rabbit hunting with me and have since he was just a couple of years old. I have taught him to watch for movement, to watch for the white bushy tails or the sun shining through the rabbit ears; to get low and stay still while you scan under bushes and next to rocks. Soon you will begin to notice that the rock you saw a minute ago is actually a rabbit, crouched low and hiding. You don't actually look for the animal, but signs of the animal, and movement. This is the key to effectively spotting game.

The reason I mention this in the introduction is that it is the first of many skills needed to be a good predator hunter. The other skills we'll get to, but "Rabbit Eyes" is something you can start to practice right away, even in your own neighborhood. You'll probably be surprised at how many animals you've never noticed, once you really start to look.

All of the information contained in this book is based solely on my own personal experiences. The techniques and tactics that I describe in these pages I have learned in the field first-hand, and they work well for me; but as the popular saying goes "your mileage may vary". I learned everything I know through trial and error, and spent some frustrating mornings out on stand trying to figure out what was going on. When I started calling, I did not know about websites dedicated to the sport; I had no one to teach me and I had read no books, but I knew there was a certain way to do it. So I picked up a predator hunting DVD featuring Randy Anderson and imitated some of what I saw in the video while I was in the field, and from there the learning began. Every season I learn more and more, and sometimes old lessons have to be re-taught! You have to keep an open mind and experiment with your calls and your tactics. More than anything, don't forget to have fun! As soon as you stop having fun, you need to find a new hobby.

Predators are crafty and are designed to stay alive, so if you don't fool them every time, don't despair. They'll slip in from the upwind side one time, come blazing by your stand at high speeds the next, and jump right into your lap at random (watch out for those foxes!). What makes the sport exciting is not knowing what's coming down the pipe at you.

So read this book, grab your calls and a good rifle, head into the wild outdoors and get ***ready for anything***!

While a friend and I were out scouting calling territory and hunting rabbits, we spotted this bobcat trying to disappear into the brush. Had we not been paying attention to our surroundings, we might have missed it.

Sometimes you have to go with a gut feeling, and try something crazy when you're in unknown territory. I tried something that went against all of my predator hunting knowledge, and it actually worked – thanks to the help and guidance of Rich Higgins, the coyote mad scientist.

I was hunting in some very unfamiliar territory with my friend Scott Francom and a very accomplished predator caller named Rich Higgins. Our first stand of the morning had produced nothing, and as we headed back to the truck, Rich and I were quietly discussing stand selection. I was expressing my concern about hunting unknown country, and he was informing me that sometimes you need to try something different, to go against the norm and throw coyotes for a loop. I asked just exactly what he meant, and he said to me "There are coyotes here this morning and they are hungry. If I said to you that I could put you on top of that hill, facing the sun, looking down into a canyon and could call something within your shooting range, would you believe me?" "Well I'd like to see that" was my reply. We hiked to the top of the hill which overlooked a big canyon and was sparse with growth on our side, and he says "Okay Glen, stand right here." Stand in the open? Are you kidding me? There was this dead tree behind me, all bent over, which barely had enough wood to allow me to lean on it, much less to hide in front of it. But I did as I was told, and prepared for an uneventful stand. Rich and Scott moved off to conceal themselves in some brush.

Rich starts his calling set and about 5 minutes into the stand this coyote just pops out of the canyon, looks right at my silhouette which I'm sure was like a beacon against the horizon, then looks in Rich's direction. Well I spare no time in putting a bullet in him and I figure that's that. Rich ends the stand a few minutes later, and he and Scott inquire what I was shooting at – they had never seen the dog. We walk over to where it was and there is no coyote. "No biggie" says Scott "everyone misses sometimes". But I knew that I hadn't – there was a solid meat report and that coyote had dropped. Or had it? After a little searching, we discovered a blood trail that was equal only to the

Nile River and was composed of little pieces of heart and lung. Somehow that coyote took a double lung and heart shot and then ran about 80 feet - pretty impressive.

My point to this story is that sometimes when you're hunting, and you're unsure of your tactics or not having the luck that you'd like; try something new, especially in an area that is new to you. Chances are it'll be new to the predators, too.

Trying new tactics that are outside of your comfort zone will often net great results.

Scouting Your Location

Just because there are coyotes in every state except Hawaii doesn't mean they cover every square inch of land, so knowing where they are and when they are there is very important. You can call all day with the perfect sound in the perfect setup and if there's no animal around to hear it, you'll strike out. Predators can be one place in the day, another at night - figure out these patterns and you'll stack the fur high.

The best way to learn is to gather as much as you can from people who know the area and then get out and hike the territory. I spend a good deal of time during the off season walking new country or checking the old spots out to make sure that they still offer good stands. If you're hunting a ranch or farm, or there are houses nearby, ask the people who live there when they see or hear coyotes the most. Some people, especially ranchers, will gladly take you right to the spot where they last saw one.

Public land offers many opportunities for hunting, and the farther in you go, the more animals you'll see. If you have access to private land, then you are sitting on a potential coyote Mecca. I have access to a small 100 acre private spot of land I hunt which produces animals 70% of the time. I don't hit it too often, but the location is perfect and no one else has access. If you can find these types of places then you will kill that many more animals.

Sometimes you have to know the right people to gain access to private land, but often it's as simple as asking. Anytime I find myself talking to a person that lives in a rural area or has some land, I always work predator hunting into the conversation. You might be surprised how many people want those blasted coyotes dead! Ask about other local landowners, and find out names and locations so that you can go out and talk to them. When you go talk to a landowner, dress appropriately so that you look respectable. You don't have to wear a shirt and tie, but clean yourself up a bit. Now I'll admit I often talk to ranchers while I'm out hunting, so I'm usually in my camouflage. But if you can, try and make an appointment to go out and see someone's land, that way they have some time set aside for you and can give you the full tour. Understand that a lot of ranchers and landowners have been let down in the past by hunters who they allowed to use their land. They have had gates left wide open on occupied pastures, had land torn up and possibly even had stock animals or pets shot. You may encounter some resistance at first, but don't let that dissuade you from trying. Tell them your desire is to hunt predators, and that you're a responsible and ethical hunter. Don't be afraid to mention the other landowners that you've worked with, as a lot of landowners and ranchers know each other. Offer to help with a project – perhaps fixing a fence or cleaning up trash along the road. If you get permission, then follow through with your promises promptly. I like to go out ASAP and kill a few yotes on the land and then take them down to the house for a little show-and-tell. As with hunting on public land you need be a responsible sportsman – leave gates as you find them, don't travel off-road, don't shoot near buildings, and don't damage property, like water tanks or signs. If you watch out for the landowner, then they'll watch out for you. I've gotten permission to hunt deer and quail no one else can, and even been offered free beef from ranchers, not to mention having exclusive access to predator hunting territory.

    So how do you properly scout? Get out and find coyote sign, listen for them howling at night, and, as mentioned above, talk to people in the area. I know a lot of people who hunt big game and see coyotes while hunting; talking to them builds my network of good coyote spots. Now get a local map and start marking all these areas you've found out about. Pretty soon, you'll start to see a pattern of where the coyotes hang out. As you continue to hunt and scout, mark the areas with the most sign and before you know it you'll have a literal road map of coyote activity. This will enable you to go out and maximize your calling time and results.

    Start keeping track of where you do stands that get responses and also which call you were using. What time of day was it? How was the weather? How did the animal react to movement or gunfire if you missed the shot? Pretty soon you will grow your 'Little Black Book of Predators' to contain enough information that it will be coveted by other predator hunters.

But what about traveling? Often I find myself in areas that I don't have the time or means to scout beforehand. If you can't scout a new location, then look for a few signs of a good stand. Look for a stand that offers animals a safe approach to your location, offers you a good vantage point of the area, offers you protection from the sun, and allows you to blend in the best. We'll talk more about this in "Stand Selection".

Get to know all of your terrain features and how animals may use them to approach your stand, such as the washes and brush lines shown in this picture

There are areas that are often overlooked by predator hunters, yet offer plenty of action and are usually close to home. Along the borders of game preserves, just outside of bird hunting farms and right outside the city limits are places where I have had tremendous success in calling animals, most of whom have never heard a call before. Research these areas and if need be obtain any permission or permits you may need to hunt them. Anyplace you can find where you are the sole hunter or one of only a few allowed to hunt a specific area will be a place that will produce many animals.

Pay extra special attention to safety and local laws while hunting close to houses and buildings. For example, in Arizona I must be ¼ mile away from any occupied structures, and I cannot shoot from, onto, or across roads. Sometimes ranches have various buildings and stock yards – make sure your backdrop is adequate for a shot before pulling the trigger. Following the rules will make sure that no one gets hurt, and that you don't end up talking to a law enforcement officer instead of spending your time hunting.

Make sure you read your hunting regulations, especially about seasons, magazine capacity limitations, and firearm limitations on certain species. Know your boundaries – don't end up in the wrong management unit, or an Indian reservation, or on private land because you failed to do your homework. Ignorance is not a good excuse when you're talking to a game warden.

When you find good stand locations, note the type of terrain. This will help you decide which firearm to bring to the stand. When hunting around urban areas or close to occupied buildings, don't discount high-powered air rifles or archery as a means to take down predators. They are lethal when used properly, produce little or no shot report, and have limited ranges. They require a little higher of a skill level to be effectively utilized, but don't let that scare you away from giving it a try.

Finding the time to hunt can be a struggle for some of us – that whole "job" thing can really get in the way. I have scouted out some stands close to my house and around the town limits, as well as on the various routes I find myself taking to job sites. You might have to get up a little earlier than normal to squeeze in a stand before work, but nothing says "seize the day" quite like a dead coyote before heading off to the daily grind!

Every now and then you have an experience that stands out in your memory whenever you think of a related topic. For me and predator hunting, it's a great morning that I had with my Dad in the fall of 2008.

It was an October morning and our first two stands had produced nothing. The sun was starting to warm us up considerably, and we had to get to my son's soccer game soon, so we decided we'd do one more stand and then call it a day.

I had called in a fox just a few weeks prior at a stand location not far away, so we drove over to the ranch it was located on and parked near a cow pasture. As we made our way up the hill to the rocky canyon overlook where the stand was located, I got a sudden rush of excitement. I told my Dad that I really thought this stand would produce something, so he'd better be ready. He sat underneath a juniper tree where he would have a good view of the canyon ledge should anything come up. He was armed with a .22 lever-action Henry, and my father is deadly with whatever firearm he chooses. Confident his section was covered, I moved closer to the ledge and farther to the east of my Dad. We were separated by about 40 yards of brush and rock. I nestled into the base of a small juniper, and my view was such that I could cover the only other entrance to this area, which was a very rocky area covered in prickly pear and scrub oak.

I began my calling with some bird in distress, and after a few minutes with no response, decided to try something a little radical. After all, it was the last stand of the day and that's when I tend to get a little experimental. I really started to get into this call, screaming loudly then softening it and then adding little whistle noises in randomly. I take a break to catch my breath and POP! I hear my Dad's .22 fire. "Perfect" I think to myself "Dad doesn't often miss, and he didn't fire again, so he got it". I start to call again to get anything else out there to come in, and not 30 seconds go by when this fox comes whizzing by my stand. I squeal loudly into the call to get the fox to stop and BAM! I let him have it with a load of buckshot from my shotgun. The fox screams and jumps into the air, then flops on the ground. I continue to call for a minute or so but then I get excited about giving my Dad a hard time for missing a shot, so I end the stand and get up.

As I am walking towards the fox, I turn to look up at my Dad, who is just kind of staring at me with this odd look. I throw my hands in the air and he shrugs his shoulders, then I say "Come and help me find this fox." He motions with his hands but I don't get it so I turn back to the task at hand. I recover the fox, and it's a big one! I pick it up proudly and turn to walk towards Dad. As he comes into view I realize he is holding the biggest fox I have ever seen! He breaks into a grin as we meet each other halfway, each of us holding a big grey fox with a beautiful late fall coat. He smiles as he tells me of how this large fox came up and over the ledge, then poked his head around some bushes to try and get a look at where I was calling from. My Dad shot him, right in the head. He never knew about the second fox until he heard my shotgun go off; turns out I shot the female on her way out, but not before she got a look at what was making all that racket. We had just taken a mated fox pair in the same stand, with each of us claiming a nice, big animal. His fox weighed in at 12 pounds, which is the largest fox I have ever seen, and mine weighed in at 9 pounds. We had a long walk back to the truck carrying two large foxes, but we also carried with us a new memory of a great hunt that we were able to share together. I have a picture of the two of us with our foxes hanging in my living room – a truly great adventure.

The Gear

Glen and Sam Stilson with their fox double – Sam's fox weighed 12 lbs!

The Gear

Hunting gear may be the most over-thought and highly discussed topic out there. Hand calls or e-caller? What pattern of camo? Which caliber of rifle? What kind of buckshot for my shotgun? Well I can't tell you what the best gear is for *you*. But I can tell you about my experiences and what works best for me.

Most guys can use what they already have to start predator hunting. A good set of camouflage, a good rifle and a call are all you need to get started – that's all I started with. Don't be pressured by popular image to run out and get the latest and greatest gear; until you know how to use it properly you're not going to get your money's worth anyway.

Wear camouflage that matches your surroundings and cover everything, including hands, face, and anything that might shine, like metal watches or rings. Patterns and designs are made to appeal to human eyes, which is not what you're after. These characteristics are not as important as are breaking up your outline, matching colors of your environment, and your ability to sit still. In my experience I have seen many guys wearing top notch camo get busted by animals because they couldn't avoid scratching their leg or repositioning their rifle. Even $500 in camo can't hide that mistake. I have even called in coyotes while wearing khaki colored pants and a green shirt - natural earth tones are better than no camo at all, but sitting still is your trump card. Make sure that you wear and wash your camo before you use it in the field – this will get rid of any factory-new smells and also get rid of that "store shelf shine." I also like to hang dry all of my camo after washing to preserve the materials and to keep out any dryer sheet smells.

I prefer the MARPAT, or MARine PATtern, digital camo. It hides me well in the area that I hunt the most, and a full set can be had for about $80. I also own a few sets of old woodland BDUs, some cheap Wal-Mart camo, and a couple pairs of pants from Vanish. I prefer the darker colors because they break up my outline better than the lighter colors. I pick my camo set for a stand based on the type of terrain I will be hunting, and also based on what is clean and hanging in the closet!

I cover my face with basic and inexpensive face masks. It's really important that a face mask be comfortable, so you don't get annoyed with it half way through a stand because it's in your eyes or making your face itch. For gloves I prefer fingerless gloves, unless it's cold and then I'll wear camo mittens. I like the fingerless gloves because it makes the manipulation of calls and firearms easier.

Ghillie suits really help to break up your outline, especially your head and neck

Ghillie suits, or leafy camo, are a great addition to any predator hunter's gear set, as they really help break up your outline; especially that dreaded 'head-neck' outline. The only real downside to them is weight and their ability to retain so much heat!

In the warmer fall and spring months I rarely wear my ghillie due to this factor. I prefer a half-sleeve ghillie so that the jute does not get caught up in my equipment. When I wear the hood up over my head I make sure the material is not hanging over my peripheral vision, that way I can catch any and all movement in my available line of sight.

Footwear needs mentioning here because it is important to choose something with adequate tread and support. You also want a pair of boots that are waterproof so as not to ruin your hunt, and not something that is all shiny, like a pair of hiking boots with reflective thread. I like to choose a boot that has a distinctive tread so I can tell if anyone other than me has been in the area recently.

I like to carry a small shoulder bag that contains my extra calls, decoys, ammo, and first-aid kit. I also carry my coyote drag, which is a length of paracord with loops on each end I can wrap around an animal's mouth or front legs for dragging them back to the truck – just make sure you drag with the direction of the fur, not against it. A bag is also handy in case you find any little 'treasures' while you're out and about. I have seen guys carry backpacks and fanny packs, even turkey or duck hunter vests – whatever works for you. I will also often carry a CamelBak when I plan on doing some lengthy hiking, or at the very least a canteen.

Decoys are not a necessity for every stand but should be a piece of equipment you always take with you into the field. In thick brush they are not very useful for the most part, and during certain times of the season they are not really needed, like when the pups are first out and about. I have tried a lot of different decoys, including white socks on fishing line, motorized cat toys, and pieces of ribbon tied to a bush. The two I have found to work best for me are the turkey feather tied onto an arrow stuck into the ground, which you can easily and cheaply make at home, and the motorized Quiver Critter from Edge products. Decoys are great for bobcats and also help those wary dogs make the commitment to come into range. I have seen animals come in locked onto the decoy, and then see me move for the shot, and continue to stay locked onto the decoy. Then again, I have seen animals take one look at that decoy and start to move away. So, as usual for predator hunting, be ready for anything.

You always want to place your decoy close to the source of your call, so obviously if you're using a digital caller then you can place it right next the unit. Using a decoy and hand calls is a little different, though. You want the decoy to work as a distraction as well as to help raise a predator's comfort level. It's been said that predators, specifically coyotes, can place a sound within 15 feet of its source. If your decoy is too far away from the sound, then the setup won't feel natural, and this will make approaching predators nervous. If it's right next to you while you are hand calling, then your movements will be seen just as easily as if you didn't have a decoy. I like to keep mine upwind from me, about 10 feet away and in front of me.

Decoys are a great addition to your toolbox - bobcats are especially fond of them.

Firearm selection is and always will be an interesting discussion. I started off with a bolt action Remington Model 700 chambered in .25-06, but it wasn't long until I saw the benefit a smaller caliber semi-auto rifle would offer. These days I prefer my AR-15, chambered in .223, and use it probably 75% of the time. I chose the AR-15 platform because of its ability for limitless customization, from scope mounts and stocks to triggers and grip configurations. I like the flexibility of a rifle – no shot is too far or too close; whereas I've been left wanting with a shotgun. My AR has been kind of a Frankenstein project for me, starting first as a 24" Bushmaster Varminter and slowly evolving to what it is now: a 16" Rock River Arms midlength carbine upper, 1:9 twist HBAR barrel, and a Bushmaster A2 lower with a DCM 2-stage trigger and Hogue rubber grip. After going through a few different scopes, I have settled on a Bushnell Trophy 4-12x42mm in an Armalite one-piece mount. Your scope mounts are important – don't go cheap here. Many good scopes are thought to be bad because of ineffective scope mounts. I also have a flip down rear sight mounted under the scope, so that if something should happen to my scope in the field, I will have backup iron sights. Hey, it's happened! I have a basic sling mounted normally under the stock but on a front sight post sling mount so I can carry the rifle across my chest or across my back. I have painted my rifle with Krylon paint in a tiger stripe pattern to eliminate glare and help break up its profile. I also like to keep some basic survival and gun care items in the A2 buttstock. I feed my AR with 55gr Remington Core-Lokt soft point rounds. I have killed predators with a lot of different rounds, from Hornady V-MAX to Winchester Silvertips, and I have found the Core-Lokts to be a very efficient and economical round.

My shotgun of choice is the very reliable Remington Model 870 Express. I added a little camo paint on the metal to keep the glare away and some camo wrap on the barrel to hide my movement. I have used a lot of different shotgun rounds, some much more effective than others, but the one I use the most right now is 3 inch #4 buckshot, which is the load I have found that gives me the most lethal range with my Remington Full choke – it contains 41 .24 caliber pellets. This load allows me to hit animals out to 60 yards. The biggest thing with shotguns is to pattern them with your selected load and choke. Different loads shoot differently in different shotguns, and through different chokes. Know what your shotgun likes to be fed and it will not let you down.

Shotguns are great for the thick brush or any areas where you expect to encounter animals at close range. They are easy to fire at moving targets or animals that would otherwise be difficult to find in a scope, like when they are standing 10 feet from you. The high pellet count of many loads means a much better chance of hitting a vital area when you are shooting fast movers.

12 gauge shotgun, 10/22 rifle, AR-15 - all with self applied camo paint

The downside of a shotgun is its limited range – I have called animals in that hang up outside of shotgun range, and then disappear, never to be seen again. These same animals would be DOA if I had a rifle in the same situation, so be aware of this downfall and choose your firearms wisely for each stand. Another downside of the shotgun is that pellets do not expand or generally fragment, meaning they do not leave large wounds through which blood can seep. If you are skinning pelts, this is great, as those tiny holes are easy to sew; but when you're tracking a wounded animal that leaves no blood trail, it can make things very difficult. I've seen those combo rifle / shotgun firearms in action and I was not impressed, but you might try carrying both shotgun and rifle to a stand in un-scouted territory – it's a heavy load but it might be worth carrying depending on your terrain.

    I like to carry a sidearm when I hunt or hike. I chose a revolver because I like the way it operates in the field and it's easy to clean, and I chose the .38 special so that I could load a powerful and economic round but also use CCI shotshell rounds for snakes. I chose the Smith & Wesson Model 64 due to it having a bobbed hammer so it won't snag on anything, and it's a very accurate pistol. I carry it in a Fobus plastic paddle holster, which retains the pistol very well while making it easy to get out in a hurry. I carry a sidearm for killing snakes, to use as a dispatch gun, and also self-defense. Calling in a mountain lion that may want to eat you is a very real possibility, and swinging a long gun around in a situation like that may not be possible. There are also too many two-legged predators out there, and you just never know when you might run across one.

    Before we get off the firearm topic, I have to say something about caliber – it's all personal opinion. Whatever you shoot well and accurately is what you want to take with you. Same goes for what brand of firearm is best, every manufacturer offers different features, choose one that fits your needs. If you want to lay waste to coyotes with your .308, be my guest, and if you want to head shoot your animals with a .22 magnum, then so be it. As long as you hit what you aim at, and take fur preservation into consideration, then use what you've got. You also need to make sure you can afford to shoot it regularly. Some calibers have spectacular ballistics, but they are so pricey that not everyone can afford to shoot a couple of boxes of ammo every month to practice.

I don't prefer shooting sticks or bipods because at the ranges I engage my animals at, which is normally under 100 yards and generally measured in feet, any type of shooting aid just gets in the way. I have shot offhand my entire life and prefer to do so. I practice this way so that I am ready for field shooting. I know a lot of guys who swear by their shooting sticks, so if you want to use them then go for it, just make sure you practice with them.

Ladders get you above the brush and allow you to see more terrain

During wet or cold seasons, I will carry a stool or cushion of some kind to keep my rear off the ground. And in thicker brush I prefer a ladder so I can get up and see more. You'd be surprised how many more animals you'll see, and I have literally killed animals mere feet away from my ladder. My friend Scott Francom introduced me to ladders a few years ago. He has even had a bobcat sit down under his while he was on top of it! They don't see you as much and you'll see more of them, for sure. I use a 6 foot fiberglass ladder painted in camo, and I really only utilize it in thicker brush, and not as much in open terrain. If you choose to use a ladder, then practice firing some shots while you're on top of it so that you're used to the recoil. Also practice tipping it over and executing a safe dismount – it's not hard, but it takes a little practice. You also want to carry it to your stands in such a way that it doesn't make a lot of racket banging together. I mounted a small strap to mine so that I can bind the legs together when I'm walking.

The use of cover scents is up to you, but I generally regard them as useless. When the animal gets downwind, they are going to smell you mixed in with the other scents, no matter what you use, but there are certainly ways to help hide it. I use the misting technique, especially in the late season. Misting is the use of a spray bottle containing a cocktail of animal urines which can be sprayed on your scent trail coming in to a stand as well as downwind from you when on stand. My personal misting recipe consists of rabbit, bobcat, coyote, and fox urine. You can generally get these ingredients from a local sporting goods store, or order them from the internet. If you'd like, harvest them yourself, but take some pictures and then let me know how it goes! Regardless of how you obtain your mist ingredients, the misting itself is pretty easy. You spray the ground where you walk when approaching a stand at locations a predator is likely to use, like a wash for example. You are to trying to confuse their senses or at least get them more interested in your calling than your scent trail. I mostly use misting while on stand, especially on windy days or at times when the wind shifts directions. A couple of sprays into the air and should a coyote, who is your main problem with scent, get a whiff of you, he may very well experience sensory overload – his brain won't be able to process all of those scents at once and he'll usually lock up. I have seen a number of coyotes stand and sniff the air when downwind from me while I line up for a shot. Misting works, but not every time and not in every situation; it's just another tool in your toolbox. And you need to be careful about carrying your mist and storing it at your house – if this bottle spills on you then you can forget about that welcome home kiss from your wife! I prefer to store my mist bottle in a coffee can in the garage, and I carry it to stand with me in its own little pouch, which is used for nothing else. The use of general cover scents, however, like the ones you spray on your body and such, are a waste of time. I have found through trial and error that having good scent discipline is much more effective. Don't wear smelly deodorant, don't shower the morning of a hunt, and don't take a rifle that smells of gun oil. This type of thinking also gets you more aware of your scent stream which will help you take out coyotes before they get downwind.

  The most controversial topic in predator calling is probably the calls themselves. There is the group that says 'hand calls only', and the group that says 'digital callers are the best'. My opinion is if it works for you and it puts the animal in front you, then who cares? I prefer hand calls and I have used them since I started calling. They don't need batteries, they can be manipulated easier, and they are small and lightweight. Personally, I don't get as much satisfaction out of a kill when I called the animal in with someone else's sounds, and I think it takes more skill to properly use hand calls. Hand calls also give you the opportunity to get the animals in really close, as they are literally headed right for you, which in turn takes more skill because since they are locked onto your location, you must be very careful with when and how you move into shooting position.

  Now this is not to say I don't use digital callers or think less of those who hunt with them. I have owned a number of digital callers, and I have killed a good number of animals thanks to them. They have their place and their uses. I like to use them in thick brush, or against educated animals. I like to use them to place animals for a good shot or sometimes at the end of a long day when I am tired of blowing my hand calls. My recommendation is to use a combination of both of them. You must also learn the limitation and capabilities of both types of calls and use that knowledge to your advantage, like knowing the range of your e-caller when it's on full volume, or knowing what temperature your closed reed hand call freezes at. Always carry some hand calls, even if you prefer e-callers, because you never know when those batteries are going to die.

A lot of guys ask which call making company is best, and that's really a personal preference thing. There are hand calls I prefer, such as the beautiful wooden calls from LeMarr Game Calls. Trust me, this is the call predators are just dying to hear, and you won't find a range of more diverse sounds anywhere else. I also like the originality and craftsmanship of Kannah Creek Calls, where you can find some of the most beautiful and distinctive looking calls I have ever seen. Sceery Outdoors makes some very unique sounding calls, and their calls are extremely durable. When I first started, I called in more animals with my $5 Tally-Ho from Tal Lockwood than anything else I ever used, and it still holds a warm spot in my heart, and often times a place on my lanyard.

Multiple calls and lanyards are great to diversify your sounds throughout the season; yet you should always have your 'go-to' calls that consistently produce.

E-callers are made from the $30 price point to the $1000 point, and money does buy quality here, but you don't need to spend the most to get the most. FoxPro and GameTraks are my #1 choices, but I have also called in animals with the $30 Cass Creek calls and the homemade Varmint Al caller. More money will generally buy you more volume and much more capability, such as dual speakers or the ability to play two sounds at once. FoxPro has the best quality sounds, in my opinion, and has callers down in the $300 range. When picking an e-caller, choose one that has remote capability, a range of at least 100 yards, a good volume array, and the ability to change the calls, like a USB port or memory card. Don't get cocky with an e-caller, though; movement, concealment, and stealth are still of the utmost importance. You also don't want to place your e-caller on the ground if you can avoid it. The sound will travel farther if your caller is placed in a bush or a tree, or on a stump or dead log or anything you can find that is a few feet off of the ground. Add a cord or lanyard to your caller and you can even hang it up if you must.

Next I'd like to say a couple of things about your vehicle. Car or truck, whatever you choose, make sure it has a few basic necessities. You need water, not just for drinking but for your engine. Predator hunting sometimes consists of slow cruising, checking terrain for stands and such, and this heats your engine up faster. Make sure you have a spare tire in good repair – this may sound basic but a good friend had a hunting day ruined last season, in the middle of a contest, because his hunting partner failed to double-check his spare. Also, have the tools necessary to perform basic repairs. Bring along some food, because you never know when that short morning will turn into an all-day trip because the action was hot. Don't drive a vehicle you're afraid to get a little bloody or dirty, and lastly, if you are going to mark your vehicle with predator hunting stickers, as I do, then park it somewhere obscure when you go to stand. If you don't, then you are advertising that location as a good predator calling spot. I had to learn that lesson the hard way.

Last but not least, we'll talk about hunting partners. Good fishing buddies consist of someone that will not hook you in the face when they cast or drink your last cold beverage. Good predator hunting buddies, on the other hand, are not so simple or easy to find. Be very careful in your partner selection. You don't want someone that will steal your good spots or give their locations away to others. Someone who knows gun safety rules and fields of fire is also very important. When you sit down on a stand with your calling partner, you need to make sure you establish which one of you will cover which part of the terrain, and always be sure to never put yourself in a position where your calling partner's section covers where you will be sitting – this is an accident waiting to happen, and treating a gunshot wound in the field is not an easy thing to do, if you get to treat it at all. A good partner must also have the same passion as you for the sport – otherwise he'll talk too loudly, slam his truck door, and move around while on stand. I have about a half-dozen guys that I will take on stand with me on a regular basis; and one of them is my father. This doesn't mean I don't go hunting with anyone else, it just means I don't take them to the good spots or expect much from them. A little presumptuous perhaps, but when you've been burned a few times you'll understand.

When you find that good hunting buddy, the guy who knows his stuff, make sure you value the time he has to offer, and learn from each other. A couple of tips on buddy hunting: don't face the same direction. Two sets of eyes means more coverage and someone always needs to be facing the downwind side to cover the 'backdoor' – you'll kill a lot of animals there. And I like to whistle or blow a call in a certain pre-determined fashion, like two short, sharp 'tweets', when I'm done calling a stand to let my buddy know it's over. I then wait for his response to make sure he's not drawing down on something when I stand up. It's also a good safety practice; you don't want your hunting partner to see movement and turn his firearm towards you. The last piece of advice is this - do not be a dog-hog. This is a surefire way to lose a good hunting partner.

Due to my odd schedule and my personal nature, I do a lot of solo calling. I enjoy calling by myself because it gives me the opportunity to collect my thoughts and depend on my own abilities. It also leaves no one but me to blame when things go wrong! Solo calling can be great fun and many predator callers enjoy it. However it can also be dangerous if executed poorly. Follow the basic rules of hiking and survival and let someone who is dependable know where you're going, what you plan on doing, and when you plan to return. I like to carry a small first-aid kit and some survival essentials like food, water, a good knife, and a way to make fire. I make sure to put lip balm and Visine in my first-aid kit, as lots of hand calling can dry out my lips and a little breeze that puts a piece of dirt or other foreign object into my eye can really ruin a hunt if I don't have a way to wash it out. I also like to carry a flashlight of some kind if I will be hunting at dusk and some disposable rubber gloves for handling bloody animals. My friend and taxidermist got blood poisoning once from handling a deer head with a blood infection – that story alone was enough to get me carrying rubber gloves. All of these items can be carried easily in pockets or small packs. Don't burden yourself with a lot of gear that you won't use, but remember: it is better to have it and not need it than need it and not have it.

A shoulder bag can carry all of your essentials into the field with you

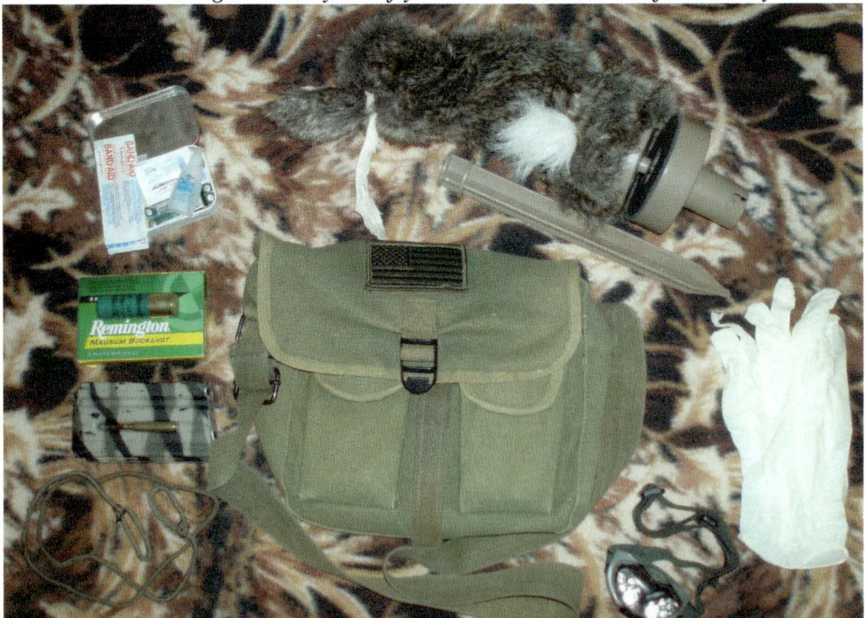

I was headed to a stand in one of my usual spots not far from my house that consistently produced coyotes. As I crested a hill I could hear the yipping of coyotes not far off and was confident I'd be able to convince one to come in. I set up next to some cat claw bushes and got settled in. Below me was a series of washes that would allow coyotes to approach the position, and I could easy maintain visibility of the entire area. Everywhere except in one direction, that is – a large tangle of scrub oak to my west. It was my upwind side so I wasn't overly concerned as I began my set.

One of the larger washes below me turned into a dry river bed about 200 yards away. Around the 10 minute mark I see a flash of fur between the bushes on the banks of the dry river bed. Expecting action, I tense myself up, ready to aim and fire in which ever direction the coyote presents itself. A few minutes pass while I continue to sing a rabbit distress serenade, and no coyote shows itself. I am beginning to relax and feel the sink of disappointment when again I see the flash of fur, headed the other direction. Somehow or another, this coyote had moved into a position from which it could observe me; probably the tangle of scrub oak on my upwind side. Not liking something it saw or heard, it was headed off – but not if I could help it. It was right around the 200 yard mark when I barked at it. For a brief moment it paused, and I thought to myself "this is a long shot, the longest I've tried on a coyote". But I held steady and fired and heard the distinct sound of a bullet hitting flesh. The coyote yelped and went down, falling near some brush. I continued to call for a few minutes, and when I ended the stand I was excited to go see this coyote, my longest shot yet. When I arrived on site, however, there was blood but no coyote. I looked around – where could it have possibly gone? The blood trail just seemed to disappear right next to the brush. As I was walking around the area, I suddenly heard a loud bark, followed by a low growl. Oh great, it's wounded and mad! I followed the barks and growls, which got louder and more ferocious as I got closer to the brush next to where I had shot the coyote. Yet I still couldn't see it. I moved back, 20 yards away where I was hoping to get a clear view and be able to deliver the finishing shot, but no luck; I could not see the dog. I didn't know how bad it was hit so I didn't know if it was bleeding out. It sounded strong yet was not moving around. I really do not like to let an animal suffer, and I knew there was only one thing to do: I got down on my belly and began to crawl into the brush, following the blood. Less than 15 feet in, I saw her. She was lying curled up against the thickest of the brush, completely hidden from my view when I was outside. She growled and barked even more now, and it was almost deafening at that distance in the confines of the thick vegetation. I managed to snap a picture of her laying there before raising myself up on my elbows, bringing my rifle up and delivering the finishing shot. It was after this that I started to carry a dispatch pistol!

Turns out that my initial shot had been a little off - the bullet had gone through both of her front legs, rendering them useless, but had missed all of her vitals. She had managed to crawl and push her way quite a distance in the time it took me to get to her. I was glad I had struck a blow that allowed me to claim another coyote, but had I taken a half a second more to aim, I might have avoided this very close encounter.

A wounded coyote will often present interesting challenges

Even a decoy couldn't get this coyote to come in any closer before I had to shoot

Accuracy Counts

Before we get to the actual calling and killing sections, I'd like to cover a little bit of accuracy information. First of all, double-check your rifle zero or your shotgun pattern a few times throughout the season - if all that calling pays off and then you miss a shot because your weapon sights are messed up, you'll be sorry.

Practice is essential during the off-season so that you can stay proficient with your firearm. I like to shoot moving targets, namely rabbits and ground squirrels. I also do some target shooting from different sitting positions. I practice shooting from my weak side, and I also do some snap shooting - I set up targets at various ranges, then snap my rifle into position and shoot them all as fast as possible, aiming for one shot kill zone hits.

Practice anatomically correct shooting – put the bullet through the front shoulder if they are broadside. This goes against the standard shooting of game animals, where we've all been taught to hold our shots behind the shoulder, but there's an anatomy difference here. The vital organs of a dog sit farther forward in their chest, and you're more likely to hit the liver if you hold behind the shoulder. While this would still kill them eventually, you want them down right now. Shooting through the front shoulder also disables them for the most part, should you find yourself tracking a wounded animal. This will change a little if they are angled and facing away from you, as a shot behind the shoulder will put the bullet right into the boiler room. If they are facing straight towards you then obviously the shot placement is straight into the chest. You can go for head shots which of course are nearly always fatal, but this takes skill (or luck) and it destroys the skull, which as you'll read later is fun to display when properly cleaned. Shoulder shots can make for a bit of a mess if you choose to skin your animals, but the benefits outweigh the hassle in my opinion.

The same can be said for foxes, but with a bobcat or a mountain lion the lungs and heart sit a little farther back, just like a regular game animal. Putting a shot through the shoulder will still stop them most of the time, but their heart sits right behind their front shoulder, which is the spot you want to hit to effectively kill them.

When sighting in your rifle, take into consideration the average distance you will be engaging targets at. I prefer to sight my predator hunting firearms in at 50 yards, as many of my shots take place well inside of 100 yards. Your terrain may be different, but overshooting an animal seems to be a common mistake.

When selecting a scope for your rifle, the same distance considerations should be taken. My scope is a 4-12x variable power, yet I rarely set it above 4x, and when I do it's usually at 6x. The higher the power setting, the harder it will be to settle the crosshairs on your target. Should an animal come close to you, as in feet rather than yards, and your scope is set to a high power, you are going to have a hard time finding the animal in your scope and making a clean shot. If an animal hangs up at a longer distance, then you can set your scope to a higher power at that time – the movement won't be noticed as much from farther away.

When you're choosing an optic for your predator rifle, you'll want to find something that offers a crystal clear picture, especially in low-light. Find a scope that is offered in a matte finish, not something shiny and reflective. Better yet, find one that is already coated or dipped in a camo pattern. As I mentioned above, a variable high power of magnification is not really needed.

I have done some coyote hunting, with good results, using an Aimpoint red dot sight. Red dots should not be completely disregarded, as some of the better ones, like Aimpoint and EOTech, can be very accurate. Many are built to military standards and will be very durable and dependable. The Aimpoint I used enabled me to easily hit a coyote on the move at 80 yards – which is really the beauty of red dots. They are great for quick target acquisition and even good for fast movers. Where the red dot is, the bullet will go.

If you're up to it, hunting with a rifle that has only iron sights offers a great challenge and helps you to practice the fundamentals of shooting. Also a good idea for areas with thick brush or heavy cover where you may have close encounters, as it's sometimes easier to find the animal in your irons than in your scope.

Using a shotgun does not mean you can just "point-and-shoot", which is the phrase so often associated with shotguns. With the types of buckshot and chokes that you will be using, you'll need to make sure that the tight pattern of shot exiting your barrel finds its mark. You'll still need to aim for the same vital areas, but the good patterns offered by a shotgun will help you to hit those areas on fast movers or close animals. I prefer to stick with the standard bead on my shotgun, but getting a high visibility bead or sight system may help you. I'm not a fan of scopes on shotguns as they limit the both-eyes-open and quick acquisition advantages of a shotgun.

There is something I would like to address here, and it is the respectability of the predator, specifically the coyote. So many people view the coyote as a varmint and a pest, which it most surely is. However, the coyote is a very intelligent creature that manages to thrive in any environment and under any circumstance. Despite their bad rap, coyotes and other predators continue to elude hunters such as us all over the nation, which should leave us all respecting them and their ability to adapt, improvise, and overcome. Coyotes, and really all of God's creatures, deserve a clean death. Take shots you know you can make, do not shoot only at 'fur', and use adequate calibers and bullets when hunting. I am not innocent of stretching my shooting ability in order to kill a predator, or taking bad shots at moving animals, but when you realize you have made a bad hit, please do the right thing and finish the job, quickly and efficiently.

As I mentioned in the "The Gear" section, whatever rifle, caliber, and bullet design you choose, you must be accurate and proficient with it. I have shot predators with all kinds of calibers and firearms, from my 9mm Beretta pistol to my Ruger 10/22. I have dusted them with a .17 HMR and turned them into jelly with my .308. It doesn't really matter what you choose, but you must be lethal with it. Practice makes perfect.

You can't always be sure how other animals will react when you are on stand, but it's good to be aware of their presence, because sometimes it can really mess you up, like it did to me in the winter of 2008.

I was hunting a private ranch that had lots of small, open pastures surrounded by oak trees and mesquite trees, providing plenty of cover for approaching animals. There are lots of cows on this ranch, and cows often come in to my setup to see what all the fuss is about, usually making lots of noise doing so. But I paid this fact no mind as I crept to the edge of one of these pastures and began my calling.

Not even one minute into the stand I see movement – a nice, sleek bobcat has begun its creep towards me. I had setup my decoy a few feet from me, and this bobcat was locked onto that shaking rabbit. The cat stayed inside the brush line, just outside of my shotgun's range, but I was confident the cat would come closer. I continued to call with lip squeaks as the bobcat began his slow and methodical approach, which is always a thrill to watch.

Suddenly, from out of the brush behind me emerges a large and agitated cow, moving her head side-to-side as she searched for the sound's origin. The bobcat locked up solid, eyes frozen on the cow that was, I am sad to say, standing directly behind me. It didn't take long for that cat to shift his gaze from the cow to the oddly shaped blob sitting beneath the mesquites. I froze, barely breathing, my shotgun still in my lap. The bobcat could see me now, and once they see you, they rarely look away. The cat sat down right at the brush line, and then slowly crouched so I could only see his ears and the top of his head. I was amazed at how the sparse yellowed grass so effectively hid the rest of his body from my sight. It was a standoff - I couldn't move, and he wasn't coming any closer.

There we sat for 5 minutes – staring at each other, neither of us moving, each waiting for the other to make a mistake. The bobcat sat at the 50 yard mark, a slim target that sitting straight towards me offered me a vital target area about the size of a fist. I had to get pellets into that fist, and quickly, but my load for that *day was 3 inch 00 buckshot in my 12 gauge, which offered me only 12 pellets, and had not proven itself beyond 40 yards. The cat's ears went back, and I knew it was game time. The cat was experiencing fight or flight syndrome, and I knew it would choose flight. As quickly as I could, I raised my shotgun and put the bead right at his head. He jumped up at my movement, and I fired, quickly racking the shotgun pump to load another round. He disappeared into the brush as I fired again, but my pellets were lost in the thick underbrush of his saving grace. I immediately jumped to my feet and ran to the spot where he had been, hoping to see blood or some sign of a hit, but there was none. I spent the next 10 minutes searching, but came up empty handed. My shot spread had been too large at that range, and with a load containing a small number of pellets, I had not scored any hits.*

So the bobcat got away to be called another day, and I left the area really wanting a hamburger made from a specific cow.

Future stand wrecker

Stand Selection

Stand location is probably the most important part of predator hunting. Where and how you setup will have the largest effect on if you call in animals and if you have the chance to kill them. If you have scouted out the area properly, then you should have a pretty good idea of where the animals are. If you haven't had the chance or desire to scout the area, then this is where paying attention to your surroundings is very crucial.

The first step is to keep it simple. Too many guys take in all of this information and then spend 15 minutes trying to analyze a location and choose a stand – I call this 'paralysis from analysis'. Use the information you have to choose the right area and then when you find a stand location that looks good, go for it. I have killed more animals following the promptings of my gut feelings than I have walking around trying to find the perfect stand. Some good criteria for a basic stand can be memorized using the following acronym. I read this in an issue of *Predator Xtreme* magazine and I have used it ever since:

PAWS

P rotection – cover + camo + no movement = hidden death
A ltitude – the higher you are, the more you can see
W ind – not in your face! A crosswind is great, and know where your downwind is
S un – at your back, at the very least sit in the shade

If a stand follows those basic principles, then it's a good stand. I also like to get a good distance away from my truck, at least 100 yards. As the season progresses, or in an area that gets hunted hard, I get even farther - sometimes I'll walk ½ mile in. The farther you walk, the better chance you have of hitting virgin territory. If you get to a stand location, though, and things are just not feeling right, then it's best to leave that stand for another day. Don't chance educating an animal or putting yourself in a bad spot when you can come back and try again another time.

Don't be scared of thick brush, either – this gives the animals extra security and enables you to hunt where others don't want to go; this is where your shotgun will earn its keep. In the thicker brush is often where I have my best success and my closest encounters.

I have two ways of locating stands when I hunt – I call them truck stands and hiking stands. Truck stands are stands where I will drive down a road, get out, walk out a ways, do a stand, return to the truck, drive down the road a ½ mile or so and repeat. You can cover a lot of terrain this way, and you get a lot more stands done in a day if you follow this method.

Hiking stands are where I park the vehicle in a central location and then hike to each setup, not returning to my vehicle for several stands or even all day. I can't cover as much terrain as quickly this way, but when I am in country that is not easily accessible to other people it allows me to reach many areas of uncalled territory. I also get to see more wildlife, more countryside, and to maintain good physical health. I do the majority of my stands while hiking, as I really enjoy the experience. I got my first bobcat during a hiking stand in an area that was heavily called by other predator hunters, but because I was over a mile from the road there is a good chance that this bobcat had not heard a call before. Based on the numbers from my 'Little Black Book', I kill bigger animals and have better encounters when I am more than a ¼ mile away from any roads.

You can base your stand setup and calling sequence on what kind of animals you expect to respond. Coyotes can be found in nearly every type of terrain. I have called coyotes in saguaro cactus lined deserts, snow-covered mountain tops, and rolling grassy hills. Foxes tend to stick to more rocky areas, where they can more easily escape hungry coyotes. They often choose to navigate via ledges and river beds. You will find bobcats in areas that have more water and thus a more ample food supply, such as creek locations and river beds. If you are scouting and see a spot that has large river trees in the middle of other types of terrain, chances are there is a bobcat nearby.

Once you find a good stand, how you sit is important. I am a right handed shooter, so I sit with my left side to the main shooting area. When sitting like this I can swing my rifle all the way from my extreme right to my extreme left. If I sit with my feet in front of me, like most guys do, then straight ahead and to my left are covered, but if an animal came in to my extreme right I would have to struggle to get there. Try it out and you'll understand.

You should call areas that may not look ideal, as this often means others have passed them up as well. This foggy stand produced a nice grey fox

In thicker brush, try ladders as I mentioned before, or stools or even stand up against a tree or tall brush. Any extra height will aid you in what you can see and how fast you can react. In more open country I spend a lot of time sitting on the ground, and I have learned you need to watch where you sit! Sitting on a red ant pile once is generally all you need to do in order to learn to check out your location. Look for snake holes or spider webs or other undesirable calling partners before you plop down. And once I discovered the excitement of chiggers, I started spraying my pant line and sock area with bug spray – in the warmer weather this is not something you want to forget.

Now that you're on stand, be quiet and sit still! I've seen a lot of good stands get ruined because guys get fidgety and make noise. Be quiet on your way to the stand, sit down, get comfortable, and don't move until you get up to leave. Then make your exit just as stealthy as your entrance, even if you kill something or miss a shot. How disciplined you are on stand depends on your desire to let ants crawl up your legs or flies buzz around your face, but I can tell you this – I have sat still through gnats buzzing in my ears and it has paid dividends when that coyote or bobcat comes creeping in.

Stand duration is up to your personal desire to sit perfectly still and be quiet, but the widely used standard is 15 minutes, and for good reason. It's been my experience that most animals respond within 10 minutes, with a few stragglers coming in the next 5. When I first started calling predators I was doing 20 and even 30 minute stands. When animals responded after 15 minutes, they seemed to come in around the 25 minute mark. However this really didn't happen that often; we're talking about 5% of stands that produced were animals that came in after 15 minutes. It didn't take me long to learn that those longer stands were mostly a waste of time. You do need to be flexible with your stand time, however, and learn to base it on terrain, weather, and season. I like to do a 20 minute stand first thing in the morning, if I'm in an area that I know has lots of animals, if it's windy, and usually the last stand of the day is also pretty long. But 15 minutes is a good starting point, and I stick to that time frame for about 90% of my stands.

Keep an eye on wind direction when you're on stand. Be aware of the wind as it shifts direction, as this will put your downwind side in a new location and you need to pay close attention for animals approaching from there. If a stand is very open I will even start out sitting with the wind to my back, that way if the animal circles downwind in the open I am guaranteed to see them. High winds are a predator hunters enemy, though – I try to avoid calling in anything above 15mph. Animals have a hard time hearing you as your calls are really only going one way, and your downwind side just became much bigger. I have called in winds up to 30 mph and had animals respond, but it makes for a miserable day and your chances of success are greatly diminished. The same can be said for calling in rain or heavy snow; however a light snow can actually be helpful, from my experience, especially in finding fresh tracks.

An easy way to check the wind en route to your stand is to carry a small eye drop container full of odorless foot or talcum powder. A couple of squirts into the air and you'll know where the wind is headed. I also use dry grass or some light, dusty dirt to verify the exact direction of the wind. When you're on stand you can't move around to check the wind, so you'll need to pay attention to grass, leaves, and other indicators that may be in the area. I tie a small white ribbon to my rabbit decoy so that when I am using it I have a great wind indicator. One of the reasons I love my feather decoy so much is that it serves as a great indicator without me having to add anything to it. As you spend more time hunting you'll begin to notice the changes in the wind instinctively while you're on stand.

Make sure you give the animals "safety routes" to your stand location - help them to feel more comfortable coming to your call. Washes, brush lines, ravines, even tall grass accomplish this. Keep an eye on these safety routes throughout your stand, and watch for movement underneath brush. During certain times of the day, such as dusk and dawn, predators are still in "safety" mode, when they feel more comfortable approaching from just about any angle. As the sun comes up and they feel more exposed, they will really begin to utilize the safety routes.

Sneak into your stand like you're sneaking your high school girlfriend back home an hour late. I can't tell you how many times I've set up shop and had animals respond in under a minute! It's stealth that will bring you that close, so watch those dry twigs and leaves on your way in. Take longer strides when you walk – only humans have short and heavy bipedal steps. As you're creeping along make sure you also watch for hazards – no need to turn a beautiful day of hunting into an emergency room visit because you stepped in the middle of a rattlesnake. Also be careful while crossing fences. Follow the rules and never cross a fence while holding your firearm, and watch out for your call lanyard – I almost hung myself once when my lanyard got caught up in some barbed wire.

    Park your vehicle where it cannot be seen from your stand location. Animals will not always be freaked out by vehicles, but that giant shine when the sun hits it sure gets them nervous. I like to sit in my vehicle for a minute to let things settle, then climb out quietly, gently shut the door, and head to the stand. Don't strain yourself trying to be quiet, but watch your path as you walk and be aware of the noises you or your gear will make, such as rubbing or squeaking noises.

    Calling the same stand is where most guys dry up their resources. They get success and so they hammer the same area until every predator within 10 miles knows the sound of their vehicle. Keeping track of where and when you call stands is how you will be able to guarantee that you're not over-hunting a location, or continuing to go back to an area that does not produce. During the early season, which is late summer and early fall, I'll hit the same area maybe twice a month to capitalize on the young animals, but as the action cools down and the season progresses, I may not see the same stand for a month or so, sometimes waiting 2 months on certain areas that offer little in the way of stand variation. But you can bet that when I head back to a good stand, some fur is going to hit the ground.

There was a feeling the morning would be very productive as I sat down on my second stand. The first stand had produced a nice bobcat and I was really looking forward to more action as I slid down a hillside and into a flat meadow. The meadow was dotted with cat claw bushes which do not make very comfortable calling positions, but I was in a good mood so I bucked up and slipped underneath one.

It was starting to get later in the season so I started with a few lonely howls. After a short pause I got into my regular routine of rabbit in distress, and very quickly there was movement. The movement was far off, about 400 yards away, and I could see two animals on a hillside among the juniper trees. They stopped moving but were clearly locked onto my position as I raised my scope slowly in order to get a better look. Sure enough, I saw two coyotes standing there, looking in my direction but making no further movements into the area. Eventually one of them moved over near a juniper and sat down on its haunches, leaving the other one to ponder its next move. Thinking that perhaps the howls brought them in, I gave another lonely howl and the coyote closest to me that was still standing took a few steps forward. This brought the coyote that was sitting to its feet, and it looked to be barking at the other one, who immediately froze and then looked back at the other, as if asking permission to proceed.

I figured I had a mated pair in my scope, but was unsure of which one was giving the orders here - male or female? I gave another lone howl and the interested coyote, who I guessed to be the male, started towards me again but was once more stopped by what appeared to be a series of barks from what I presumed to be the female. Not knowing how to end this little 'domestic dispute' I figured I'd try to get the attention of the female – if I could get her to come in, then he would surely continue his approach. I proceeded to let loose with a series of puppy yips and coyote-in-distress sounds that were loud and desperate; it did not have the desired effect. Instead, they looked at each other and promptly trotted up and over the hill, disappearing from my sight.

Call Sequence

    Well I couldn't let that be the end of it, so I picked myself up and literally ran the ¼ mile or so to the position where I last saw them. When I arrived on the juniper covered hillside, I quickly caught my breath and sat beneath a tree. Howls weren't working and neither were coyote or rabbit distress. There were some scattered houses in the vicinity, so I figured I'd give cat-in-distress a try. I gave my best imitation of a cat pleading for death and in less than 2 minutes that male was charging towards me. I raised my rifle and dropped him in his tracks, saw movement to the left and, moving my head away from the scope, saw the other coyote, the female. She was standing about 200 yards away on another hilltop, looking towards me and her now dead companion as if to say "I told you so!" before she dropped over the hillside and was gone.

Offering an educated coyote a different sound will help you seal the deal.

Call Sequence

Probably the second most discussed topic in predator hunting is call sequence. Some say you need to have pauses, some just scream endlessly until something shows up or the stand is over. I have heard guys say you shouldn't change sounds in the middle of the stand, and heard others say you should give the animals whatever they need to hear. In reality it all works just fine as long as there is an interested animal out there.

I like to use a couple of different calls during a stand, as coyotes often respond from curiosity and may need to hear something a little different to be interested.

Calling sequence for me depends on the time of the year. When I'm in thicker brush I generally start low and slow and gradually raise the frequency and volume. I start low so as to not scare away animals that may be close-by, and I end high to bring in those far off animals. If I'm in big country I usually just blast the call throughout the whole stand. You need to be careful doing this if you are using hand calls as some hand call reeds can be overblown and reeds can even get busted when you are blowing too hard. I like to avoid long pauses in sequence to ensure I keep the attention of any cats in the area, as they get easily distracted and will pursue other interests.

  Pausing in your sequence, as I mentioned above, is an oft discussed topic around the campfire. I can't say I've had any real experience where pausing or not pausing made a difference. I have an idea that a responding predator would like to continue to hear the screams of his prey to make him more motivated to get to the call before one of his fellows does. I also have the idea that a dying rabbit can't scream all day. And since I do most of my calling with hand calls, it's not very easy to constantly scream when I've got limited lung capacity. So I give some pauses on most setups, short 30 second or so pauses keep the animal interested and allow me to catch my breath. This is usually after about 3 or 4 minutes of calling, during which I'll be changing volume and tone to replicate an animal that is actually dying. Remember that an animal doesn't get to practice dying, so as long as you sound in pain and scared, you'll be good to go.

  I won't say I've ever done this on purpose, but during the course of rabbit hunting I have wounded a few rabbits. I have often had the opportunity to hear them scream in distress, and I have to say it generally doesn't sound anything like the racket I make on stand! Oh sure they scream and wail and thrash about, but it's not prolonged and it certainly isn't as loud as the sounds I make. It is usually a low volume moan with some squeals and squeaks thrown in. I have also sat down nearby to wait for an incoming predator, but have never had the opportunity to kill a coyote coming into the sound of a real dying rabbit. The predators that I have killed don't seem to know the difference, and they are still coming to our reproduced calls, but it does say something about the replication of natural sounds. Often I wonder just exactly what the coyote or bobcat or unsuspecting fox was hoping to find when he showed up. With all that loud screaming, it must be rabbit-zilla!

During the winter and into the new year, I like to start with some howls, though I stick to the basics with coyote vocalizations as it's easy to send the wrong message. Lone howls, or locator howls, are long drawn out howls, usually starting with a couple of barks. A challenge howl is a much shorter version of a lone howl, and is meant to draw out the males for a territorial fight. I don't challenge howl a lot, as it can tend to scare off some of the younger dogs. Other than that it's all distress of one kind or another. I'll often end with a pup or coyote-in-distress - it really does make a difference for those call-shy animals, and it's great for the early season when the coyote adults are still looking after their young. Which distress you choose for the bulk of the stand is a roll of the dice, unless you have been keeping track of your stands in your 'Little Black Book' in which case you may know exactly what to use. If you are targeting a certain animal then you may also start with a certain sound which appeals to them. I like to find what works in an area and stick to it until it doesn't work anymore. I change the calls on my lanyard, with a couple of exceptions, throughout the season so I always have a fresh sound to offer an area.

When I'm on stand and I've been calling for 10 minutes or so and nothing is responding, then I'll try something else, usually something different or a sound I haven't been using in the area. During the early season, I like to go with some pup-in-distress, but I'll also often use fox-in-distress or cat meows or just get really wild with a rodent distress. Three sounds per stand is my limit – you don't want to throw the whole toolbox at them all at once. If you have an animal that hangs up out of range and doesn't seem interested, throw them a couple of different sounds at different tones or volumes and see if that peaks their interest. Most of my animals are called in with some kind of distress, with rabbit leading the way and bird in a close second, followed by pup and fox in distress.

One of the best sounds that you'll ever use requires no purchase at all – the lip squeak. Once an animal starts to approach, I like to stop calling and lip squeak them in, which basically still sounds like a whimpering rodent or other prey. I make a fake kissing sound with my lips, and I have even seen guys kiss the back of their hand to make the sound. Either way, you should practice it a little before you head to stand, and only use it once they start to close in.

If you happen to be utilizing either a calling partner or a digital caller, then sometimes you might want to try dual calling. On stands where you know there are animals but they are not responding, such as with educated animals, or even just for fun at the end of a long day of hunting, I will have a calling partner make one type of distress while I make another. You can do this with a digital caller just as easily, and actually have more control over the situation, but I like to hear what my calling partner is going to throw out there. Howling this way is extremely effective – you can make it sound like a whole group of coyotes, or even turn it into a coyote fight other dogs may rush in to see.

Hand calls can be challenging to master, but can also provide some very close encounters – these two foxes were shot on the same stand less than 20 yards from me.

If you have seen any predator hunting videos, then you have seen those hunters bark when they want a coyote to stop. This is a pretty basic concept, and will work for foxes, as well. Simply bark a nice solid WOOF and they will generally freeze to the spot, allowing you a nice still target, but they won't stand there forever. I have used a loud lip whistle to the same effect.

Hand calls can range from the most basic to the most beautiful. Above, left to right, are the 'Tally-Ho' from Tal Lockwood, the 'Hi-Jacker' from LeMarr Game Calls, and an antler and wood open reed call from Kannah Creek Calls. These are some of my 'go-to' calls

If you go the hand call route, you may want to start with a closed reed call before jumping into open reed calls. Open reeds will give a better sounding call, and allow you to vary the sound more, but closed reeds are easier to blow. Some open reeds can also be used as howlers as well as distress. Either way, if you think you sound crazy blowing into that thing, here's a tip: make your call sound like a crying baby. Blow into it and try to get a kind of 'wah-wah' sound. Vary the tone and frequency for best results.

Learn to 'shake' your vocal chords and you'll get a great sound. Flick your tongue like you're rolling a Spanish 'R', only much faster, and you'll get a bird sound. Go ahead, experiment with that hand call, though I recommend doing it in your truck or your garage, somewhere far away from your spouse! And this may sound a little weird, but it's how I learned to get into the groove - imagine you're a dying animal when you call. Seriously - that's what works for me. It helps you put more emotion into it, and helps you to sound genuine and to get those educated dogs to come trotting in. It also helps you to avoid sounding like everyone else that's blown a call in the area.

 Knowing a little about acoustics and how sound travels when you're calling is a great advantage, and you can learn a lot about how your sounds travel just by utilizing either a digital caller or a calling partner. You'll need to do some experimenting in different terrain, such as valleys, close-in hills, open prairie, mountain tops, and any other terrain you might encounter. If you don't know how far your call will reach when you're in certain areas, then you don't know how far you need to travel before your next stand or how far potential animals may have to travel to reach you. Most of the time, your calls can be heard ½ mile or even up to 1 mile away, but calling in areas with big terrain features like rocks and hills and dense forest can affect how far and where your sound travels. I have sat on stands where I could barely hear a calling partner, and I have called on stands in valleys where it sounds like the call echoes for miles.

 When you are on stand and especially when you're hand calling, you need to be aware of your head movement. You can't just sit there and scan the area with your head on a swivel – you need to make small and deliberate movements. I like to sit down on a stand and determine my biggest field of vision, then look into the center of it, moving my eyes right and left and covering as much terrain as possible without moving my head. When I need to look in a new area, I slowly turn my head towards it while continuing to scan for movement. You don't want to take too long doing this as you don't want to miss an incoming animal – I can usually complete a whole 180 degree scan of my area is about 30 seconds. Turn your head slowly towards any animals, as jerking your head towards movement is a great way to giveaway your position. The same can be said when you are hand calling – I have learned the hard way to limit my hand and head movement while hand calling. You pretty much have to move your fingers and hands around to grab different calls or to manipulate calls to get a different sound, or to punch buttons on your e-caller remote. But there is really no need to rotate your head around while calling. The sound is traveling out in every direction, and you moving it a few inches either way is not going to help it go in any one direction more than the other.

Crows respond to a lot of stands. When they are in season, don't discount them as varmints!

I've talked a lot about coyotes, foxes, and bobcats, but have not discussed other predators. The three above, or the 'trifecta' as they are sometimes called, are the most common that you will see on your stand. But there are others that will show their faces occasionally, like badgers, raccoons, and even mountain lions.

We'll cover mountain lions first, one of my most sought after goals. When you find mountain lion sign, such as fresh scat or track, set up nearby. Standard distress calls will work, but if you have the ability to make the sounds of a larger wounded game animal, such as a fawn, then use this to your advantage. Mountain lions have a large range, said to be up to 50 square miles, so don't be disappointed if one does not show its face.

Mountain lions can take some time to show up, with some hunters reporting they were on stand for up to an hour, but a lot of callers who get them report that their lion seemed to show up rather quickly, generally inside of 20 minutes. Targeting lions is difficult, but certainly possible, and there are a few good books and videos out there featuring lion experts that will show you the ropes. In my experience with trying to call lions, the most difficult part is not shooting the coyotes and other predators that show themselves while you're sitting there trying to hold out for a big cat!

Badgers are kind of a treat on stand. You won't see them often, but when you do, it's fun because they are so ferocious and generally have a bad attitude. They respond really well to bird-in-distress calls and other high pitched sounds, but do not exclude other sounds from your setup if you're trying to get a badger. Your best bet for seeing badgers is to locate an area where they have been seen, as they do not have a large range. Look for their recently excavated dens when you are walking to your stand, and call the area in the morning, when they are finishing up their hunting.

Raccoons can be found near riverbeds, creeks, and almost any running water source. They respond pretty quickly and move fast, so if you see one then be prepared for quick shots. Like badgers they seem to prefer the high pitched sounds. If you happen to setup near their home, they might appear in trees or logs as they begin to approach but you need to let them clear that opening before shooting to avoid wounded or dead animals falling back into a dead tree and preventing you from retrieving them.

Any movement while you're on stand seems to instantly get your heart pounding - but remember target identification and fields of fire! These horses came to check out all of the noise and then stuck around for the entire set.

Be aware of bear activity in your calling locations as well. I have only had bears respond a couple of times, and they were black bears which for the most part are not dangerous. But if you should find yourself between a mama and her cubs, or a really hungry bear decides to get right in the middle of you, you could have a bad situation on your hands. The bears I have called in have all approached to a distance of less than 10 yards from me, and it really is neat to see a bear up close and personal like that. But 10 yards is the limit of my comfort zone for an animal of that size so a little wiggling around was all that was needed to scare them off. I have continued calling on stands after a bear has left but I have never had anything respond post-bear. Black bears really seem to like very raspy noises, but a high or low tone doesn't seem to matter. Some states, like Arizona, have an over-the-counter fall season bear tag that can be purchased fairly cheap, but be aware of things like harvest limits and mandatory check-ins.

All kinds of animals will respond to your calls, mostly out of curiosity, such as deer, antelope, hawks, owls, ravens, rabbits, cows, javelina, domestic dogs, etc. Be sure of your target before you pull the trigger, but also be ready for some action! I had a yellow lab come up behind me and bark, which about made me wet my pants. Another time I was hunting with my good friend Fred and he had a red-tailed hawk land on his rifle barrel as it rested on his shooting sticks. I have been dive-bombed by falcons and owls, and had deer nearly run me over. Javelina get really annoyed because a cottontail screaming sounds a lot like a baby piglet, and I have had boars come in to grunt and paw the ground a few yards in front of me. Rabbits will often respond to rabbit-in-distress, sometimes standing up on their back legs to look at you, sometimes they even seem to do a mock charge! Cows often get very interested in your calls, sometimes too interested, and sometimes the mama cow gets WAY too interested – does running from a cow make me a sissy?

The sun had been up for quite some time as I settled into another stand. I was seated on the side of a small knoll, overlooking some washes and brushy country. The morning had only produced one coyote that was too far away for a good shot and was more interested in wherever he was headed than coming over to check out the crazy noise. I was planning for a few more stands before heading home, so I pulled my face mask up over my face and settled into position, resting my rifle as always across my right knee and left foot.

I began to scream some distress into the air. Some time had passed before I took a pause, and as I was scanning the brushy valley floor below I saw a jackrabbit dart from its hiding place and race off elsewhere. This usually means good things are about to happen and I was happy to see a coyote break out of the brush and come running towards me, giving a slight look at the escaping rabbit but paying more attention to me, his hoped-for easy meal. This coyote was easily 200 yards away and headed straight towards me, so I shifted my position once he was behind some brush so that I would get a nice, steady shot at him when he came out.

The knoll I was sitting on had a kind of cliff at the end of it, so much so that I couldn't see the bottom of it from my position, but not so much that the coyote couldn't climb it with ease. As I waited for him to break into view, to fill my already steadied rifle scope with a great shot opportunity, I caught movement out of the corner of my left eye, and turning my head I saw my coyote, who had clearly decided not to climb up in front of me but rather take an easier route. He saw me move at once and just as fast as he appeared he was gone. I had moved into position too quickly, assuming that I knew what an often unpredictable animal was going to do.

Animal Behavior

There is a lot to be said about why predators behave the way they do, why they respond to certain calls and not others, and how their behavior while in or out of your line of sight can directly affect your ability to put fur on the ground. I can't hope to cover all of it here, but I will touch on some basic principles.

Coyotes, in particular, are opportunists. They are compelled by hunger, curiosity, territorial instinct, and essentially greed. They do not want to be the last to the dinner table, nor do they want someone else getting their share. In his book *Roughing It* Mark Twain described the 'cayote' as "a living, breathing allegory of Want. He is always hungry. He is always poor, out of luck and friendless. The meanest creatures despise him and even the flea would desert him for a velocipede."

Coyotes learn from their experiences and mistakes, and they learn quickly. It is this principle that makes educating them to the ways of the human hunter such a hazard to our sport. Some animal researchers have even speculated that coyotes teach their young how to avoid the pitfalls of man. So when you educate one dog to the dangers of your call, you may have just taught the future generation, as well.

Hunger is obviously a motivation for predators due to their need to constantly be on the hunt. Appealing to their hunger side will not always prove productive in every season – winter time will find the hunter without as much prey, whereas in the summer the prey is ample and they can hunt during the day and at night due to the warmer weather.

Predators may not always be responding to distress calls due to hunger, however. Curiosity could very well be the number one motivator to get animals to come in. I say this because so many other animals come in on stands, from deer and javelina to cows and even rabbits, none of which are interested in eating meat, but may just want to see what's going on in their neck of the woods. Some distress calls sound similar to a fawn-in-distress, or a piglet-in-distress, and therefore some animals may be responding out of their instinct to protect their young, which is why we use pup-in-distress calls to lure in coyotes. Predators may be responding to check out a meal location for later, or even to "play" with their prey, as a form of amusement. During your calling sequence, it is important to use sounds that may stir a predator's interests, such as an animal it hasn't heard before, like a piglet-in-distress where there are no pigs. Predators that respond through curiosity may not always come running in. They may stay inside their comfort zone of the brush line or wash, observing and deciding their next course of action. This is why sitting still is so important – if you do not limit your movement then it is easy to spook a predator that is just out of sight, and then you'll never even know you called them in.

Territory is an important factor to consider when choosing your stand and calling sequence. Coyotes generally have an established territorial zone, which they will defend adamantly if they feel threatened. Coyotes are also communal animals, and will come around just to say "hey" to another coyote, or to check out potential mates. I have read that bobcats center their territory around one female in an area, meaning there are multiple males in the area. Killing the males will continue to bring more males into the area, while killing the female may or may not bring another female in immediately, meaning that the males may seek mating territory elsewhere.

Knowing a predator's territorial zone is not really required for you to be able to call in animals, but be aware of how many males and females you take out of an area. This information, over time, will help you to take a guess at the breeding potential of the region. This will then help in next year's scouting and stand selection.

In my experience, foxes make themselves scarce in coyote country. They choose to stay close to rock formations and outcroppings, cliffs and brushy undergrowth, so as to be able to escape their #1 predator – the coyote. Using fox-in-distress around potential fox spots is a near surefire way to draw out most foxes or lurking coyotes in the immediate area.

Be ready for non-predator species to react to your calls, sometimes in a hostile manner. The javelina pictured above, slightly obscured by some grass, was hackled up and angry when it responded to a set of calls that one of my calling partners made on our way to a stand. It left only after some heavy convincing.

Greed seems to penetrate every species in the animal kingdom. New coyote pups recently kicked out of their dens suddenly find themselves in direct competition with their brothers and sisters. Human expansion into animal territory increases predator numbers in an area not ready or capable to support a larger population, therefore competition and greed can entice predators in and around suburban areas and new housing developments to respond to calls more quickly and aggressively than they may have in other areas where the prey is more abundant.

Prey types and predator species in the area will have an effect on the type of calls you use, and even how you might setup your stand. For example, if you are calling an area where there may be foxes, you might try some bird noises or small rodent noises, and avoid the screams of larger prey or excessive coyote howling. Bobcats seem to respond to all distress noises, but I have had the greatest success using bird and cottontail distress. I have heard that howling will scare off bobcats, but in my experience that is not so, as I have had bobcats respond to distress calls just minutes after I finished howling. Decoys will earn their place in your hunting bag when you are in a bobcat area. Nearly every bobcat I have called seems to come in more quickly when a decoy is present in my setup.

Mountain lions are a predator I do not have much experience in calling. There are a few real experts on the topic of mountain lion calling, and these men and women seem to call 8 to more lions every year! For the rest of us, calling in a cougar seems to be a stroke of luck. I personally know just a few predator callers who have obtained this "crown jewel" of predator hunting by successfully calling in and killing a cougar. Yet a majority of them were not targeting mountain lions; one just happened to show up. This is why I always carry a mountain lion tag with me when I go on stand!

When you find yourself in mountain lion country, pay special attention to your setup. Do not back up to anything that does not provide adequate protection from a rear approach, such as small bushes or light, leafy cover. This is especially important when you are hand calling, as the animal will be approaching your exact location and cats prefer to approach their prey from behind, so as to maintain the element of surprise.

Animals on the approach will often give you indications of what they are about to do next. The following observations are based on my experience, and you may observe different behaviors, so pay attention to how animals are acting when they respond to your calls.

When I see a coyote that, while coming in, continues to look over its shoulder, then I expect a double or a different animal to be coming in as well. I try to let the first animal get as close as I can before taking the shot to make sure I don't spook off his companion or any other incoming predators. Other animals will look at incoming predators as well, and their behavior should also be an indication of what's about to happen. I have had cows suddenly turn their heads and watch an incoming coyote, and I have had deer that were once peacefully grazing suddenly go on alert and then dart into the brush. You will often see rabbits or birds flushed from bushes and trees as predators approach, giving you an indication of their direction. Birds will generally go nuts squawking and tweeting when they catch sight of an approaching bobcat, and larger birds like crows or hawks will dive-bomb incoming predators to try and keep them away from a potential meal.

I'd like to add a bit on the topic of cows. There are still plenty of people out there who make their living from raising cattle and other livestock. Lost or damaged livestock can really hit a rancher in the pocketbook. When you are on stand and cows or other livestock are present, try not to get too close to them. If you are hunting private land, don't make calls or movements that alarm the cows, as the rancher is really not going to like you harassing his livestock. Be aware of your shooting zones – coyotes will sometimes approach from within the cows. Do not shoot or even raise your rifle until they are in open country. Watch your fire, because when the adrenaline hits and the shooting starts, you don't want to swing too far and accidentally shoot an animal you didn't intend to.

Sometimes you will see a predator who, after posting at a location, will stare hard in your direction, then look behind themselves or in another direction. Looking around after posting generally means they are about to leave. They feel something isn't right, or they have seen or heard something out of place. This is especially evident when they lay their ears back; it's time to take the shot or you will potentially miss the opportunity. But if the animal continues to appear comfortable and relaxed, then let it keep coming. Why shoot it at 80 yards when you can shoot it at 18 feet? Until it gives you reason to believe otherwise, enjoy the show and learn from its behavior as it works its way towards you.

Not all animals you encounter will be scared of you – these badgers were not pleased to discover I was a human, and the encounter nearly turned into a case of self-defense!

    I was on a stand where a grey fox was making his final dashing approach towards me when he suddenly froze and looked hard to his left. He crouched low in the grass and then sprang to his feet and bolted off, fast as he could. Left scratching my head about what had happened, I almost didn't see the coyote as he came charging in from my right. Coyotes will kill and eat foxes and that particular fox did not want to be anyone's meal.
    Animals that hang up well outside of range, such as animals that stare at you from 400 yards away, are generally

educated animals, but may just be uninterested in what you have to offer. They will need to hear something really different to want to come any closer. Educated animals present a special challenge for the predator hunter, as they have been shot at or called to and then busted the hunter, meaning they now know the game and will be that much more cautious. Educated animals are tough to call in, but doing so will reward you with a certain satisfaction. I once spent two weeks hunting a certain pet-killing female coyote. Another hunter and I alternated calling on stands and yet every time we caught a flash of fur or a distant shape on the horizon, she would move on before offering any type of shot. Then one day, while hunting solo, the other hunter decided to use a combination of cat-in-distress and pup-in-distress, played simultaneously and at low volume on his digital caller, to coax her within rifle range, which she clearly did not believe was 150 yards. He made a well-placed shot and pets in the area have been thanking him ever since.

Interpreting coyote vocalizations is a book all on its own, and in fact there are some available out there on the topic. You'll find predator hunting websites teeming with people who will debate to the bitter end whether or not a human will ever properly understand coyote talk. As I mentioned in "Call Sequence", I limit myself to just a couple of coyote vocalizations, for fear of sending the wrong message. However, there is one coyote sound that is recognized easily, and one that can be imitated fairly easily, as well. It is the threat bark, and the threat bark is the bane of the predator hunter's existence. This sound is best characterized as a short bark followed by a few yips and then a few more short barks. It is the game over buzzer for the most part. The coyote has smelled you, seen you, or just knows something isn't right, and he's going to tell everyone about it. Unless you have him in sight, you probably won't ever see him, and only once have I ever gotten a "barker" to continue to come in. That was with a *heavy* set of pup-in-distress noises. This is a good time to test your calls, or just have some fun swapping "fightin' words" with a song dog.

Here in the West we face something every year in our predator populations that makes them act a little crazy, and that's rabies. Rabies has been responsible for 2 bobcat and fox attacks on people this last year right here in my town. Just over the mountain in another town there was even a bobcat that walked into a bar! Sounds like the start of a good joke, but it actually happened and a man inside got attacked. There were many more rabies attacks from predators around the state, including a mountain lion that attacked a young boy in the midst of a group of people on a family ATV ride. Luckily his uncle had a handgun and was quick to react, killing the mountain lion and saving his nephew.

    It's near impossible to tell just from looking at an animal if it has rabies, especially from a distance. I have killed a few animals, all of them foxes, who have turned out to be rabid. I'm no scientist but I can tell you a few red flags in their behavior that I noticed. I have had other hunters confirm my observations of rabid animals they have killed.

    Odd behavior such as wandering around like they're lost, even when responding to a call, is a good first sign. If you are walking to a stand or you are on stand and encounter an animal that is abnormally aggressive, or that does not seem to be afraid of you, there is a good possibility it is rabid. I shot a rabid fox once that appeared to be almost drunk, like it couldn't stand up properly. It's important not to touch an animal you think may have rabies, which is one of the reasons I carry disposable gloves to stand - I hear the rabies shots are not too pleasant. If I feel an animal may have rabies or be otherwise infected, I do my best not to touch them, no matter the quality of pelt, and leave them for nature to dispose of. If you shoot an animal and things get a little bloody, try to handle them by whatever body part isn't covered in blood, like an ear or leg. Be careful when handling them by the tail, as animals often urinate and defecate when you shoot them, and you don't want that all over your hands. I work in a profession where my hands get all scratched up so I often have small cuts on my hands, and I have to be very careful to not get anything "undesirable" into those open sores.

    There are other behavior indicators you will need to be on the look out for in your area. Watch the animals in your hunting zones, learn their language, and you will become a more efficient hunter.

My hunting partner Kelly Lewis and I believed this grey fox to be rabid due to its behavior. It wandered around like it was lost and then hissed and growled at us before I shot it. Even though I grabbed it by the very end of the tail, I probably shouldn't have handled it at all.

My good friend and calling partner Scott Francom shared the following story with me about what he described as being "surrounded by coyotes".

"I am lucky to live adjacent to vast amounts of desert teaming with desert wildlife. During the off season I take time to enjoy Arizona's predator population by taking pictures of them with my Canon Rebel xTi digital camera. Interestingly I have found it much more of a challenge getting a coyote into the camera's lens than into my Burris scope reticle. One morning I got up early and packed my camera gear and caller back into the desert mountain range behind my home. I have seen and heard coyotes in the area and knew that if I was patient I could get some good pictures of a coyote or two, especially since it was denning season and I planned on using some coyote pup distress sounds from my GameTraks caller.

"After hiking back in a good mile or so I settled into the backside of a nice canyon with gradually sloping canyon walls. In front of me was a giant valley four to five miles wide and thick with vegetation. I put on my ghillie suit and set up my camera tripod with my caller some 20 yards down the slope in front of me. I had backed up against a 4 foot tall creosote bush to break up my outline to the early evening sun. I began with female coyote howls spread about 2 minutes apart. After about 5 minutes I switched to coyote puppy whines and immediately the valley came alive with movement from one side of the valley to the other. I had a pair of coyotes walking toward me from directly in front of me about 200 yards out. They were at a fast trot and never posted up as they wove through the brush and trees. Closer to my caller came a nice sized coyote at a full run. He closed the distance quicker than the others so I quietly and with a minimal amount of movement panned my camera lens toward him. I began clicking the shutter when he approached the caller at 25'. I got 4 good pictures before he heard the camera and turned tail and retreated back about 100 yards then sat down and began just staring at me. Suddenly I remembered the 2 coyotes that were at a walk. One of them had *stopped at about 75 yards and was trying to get a good look at the supposed coyote pup whining from within the brush. The second, more bold coyote circled the canyon wall trying to get downwind of the caller, which would put him smack dab in my lap at the route he was taking. I held my breath as this coyote walked 7' to my right staring down at the caller. My Canon 300mm telephoto lens was pulled all the way back but was unable to focus on an object so close so I just laid there on my side looking at the coyote as he sniffed the air at different levels. Finally a slight movement on my part caught his eye and he retreated back 30 feet to an outcropping of rocks and for the next 40 minutes stared at my ghillie clad figure. I am sure he didn't know I was a human and the moving form combined with the puppy whines and distress intrigued him to no end. What I guessed was that his mate was still sitting in front of me along with the hard charger. They were only 50 yards apart but seemed unaware of each other. As I sat clicking pictures of these 2, I saw 2 more coyotes crest a rocky saddle to my left. As they came down into the valley they saw the other coyotes and gave them a wide berth. One was bolder than the others and came down to the caller, passing about 30 feet in front of me. I snapped a score of great pictures of the coyote, who didn't appear to know I was there. He approached the caller and circled it a few times and then, catching a whiff of my scent on the caller, headed back to his companion. These two meandered back and forth to my far left along the canyon wall for close to 15 minutes. After 30 minutes of coyotes all around me I actually began to grow anxious and I started wondering what they would do if I just stood up. I slowly got to my knees and then to my feet and looked around. The coyote on the rocks behind me began threat barking and acting agitated. The 2 to my left began crawling up the mountain to their rocky saddle and the 2 below me got to their feet and milled around. I caught another coyote I had never seen run off from about 75 yards away. Somehow he had crept up and I never even saw him. I snapped a few more photos of coyotes in the different stages of heading out and began my walk back out of the valley. After walking a few hundred yards I pulled off my ghillie suit and looked over my shoulder and saw a fantastic picture of 3 coyotes all silhouetted against the desert sky. They were all very much aware of where I was and my actions and were almost keeping an eye on their valley until I had left. 2 weeks later I went back with a friend who also is an avid wildlife photographer with hopes of replicating this spectacular event. With 2 guys taking pictures we were bound to have a plethora of stunning photos. After 45 minutes of calling we saw 1 coyote at 300 yards and he instantly began threat barking until we packed up and left. If I hadn't taken the pictures the first time I don't think any one would even believe that it had happened.*

"*Interestingly I have been out to this area for over 3 years with my rifle and have hardly ever seen a coyote. I take my camera and I see more coyotes in one place than I ever have in my life. I feel fortunate that I was given this opportunity to enjoy the company of coyotes up close and personal.*"

Shooting predators with a camera can still prove to be a challenge . . . .

. . . . but it can be equally rewarding!

Seasons

In Arizona I can kill coyotes year round, though bobcats, foxes, badgers, and raccoons all have a season, which I normally use as the guidelines for my typical calling season – first of August to the end of March. Mountain lion season falls in there, too, from the beginning of September to the end of May. I always get out in May and June and try to hit the coyotes during the birthing season, which I'll discuss later. Other than that, unless I have a problem coyote I get a phone call about or I just really get an itch to do some calling, I try to stick to my season. I like to take it easy on pups and not kill their parents while they are still tending to the den. I also try not to kill too many pups before they are grown, or damage the next season's potential by hunting too hard during the denning period. Not to mention that during the summer, it's just too hot to sit out there on stand! I do like to go out in the late summer and howl to dogs, just to locate them, maybe even call a few in and mess with them a bit, you know - try out calls and experiment with decoys and such. But you have to be careful – you don't want to educate them too much!

If you're not having any success in getting animals to respond, it might not have anything to do with your calling ability. If there are no animals in the area, or no animals are interested in your call, then you'll have nothing show up. Plus there's the frustrating knowledge that you've probably called some in and just never seen them - it happens plenty of times. Remember that just because an area has sign doesn't mean the dogs are ready to run in and die – if an area has been called a lot and the animals have been educated, it's hard to get them in. You might have to try new tactics. Get creative with what you do, pull something off they haven't seen or heard before, and you just might get to bag an educated animal, which is a real treat.

Certain seasons will present rapid weather changes that can prove very useful in improving your overall predator hunting success. When you have rainy weather that sets in all night long, you can be sure there will be good calling opportunities in the morning, as the animals have been holed up all night long, trying to stay dry. When there is a rain or snow storm that suddenly breaks in the middle of the day, I always try to get out and do some hunting as quickly as possible. The animals will be out and about, taking advantage of the break in bad weather in order to secure a meal. A sudden cold front moving in after a lot of hot weather, a nice sunny day after a cold, snowy one, or even the brisk evening chill that sets in when the sun goes down after a warm day are great opportunities for you to get out there and take advantage of some empty stomachs.

There are seasons that other animal species follow that present the predator hunter with great opportunities. When cows are calving, coyotes will hang around the area, often in large numbers. They will utilize the pack mentality to take down larger calves. The same event occurs when big game animals are giving birth, such as elk, deer, and antelope. I have seen coyotes literally hang around an antelope herd while does were preparing to give birth. The coyotes will bide their time, waiting for the right moment to strike. When that moment comes, there will usually be one coyote that antagonizes the doe from the front, keeping her attention from her fawn. Two or more coyotes will attack the doe from the rear, quite literally pulling and ripping the calf out of the mother. It's a fairly gruesome sight, and when it's all over the calf is generally dead and sometimes the mother is, as well. Another tactic they like to use is to have a couple of coyotes chase the doe from an area while other coyotes search for the fawn. Once found, they all join in the meal, and the doe is hopeless in defending her young. Coyotes execute the same maneuver against cows, elk, and deer. A rancher that I hunt for had a bull calf taken down by what we guess was about four coyotes, working together as a team. It's only during this birthing season that I have seen coyotes operate as a pack, like wolves.

Taking down coyotes during this time can really help your local big game populations. Here in Arizona the coyotes have taken an extensive toll on the antelope, which used to be very plentiful and are now really suffering in a lot of regions throughout the state. Hunting during these times will not only increase your chances for multiple animals on a stand, but will also have you participating in hunting's primary role, which is conservation. If you are on private land and are taking down calf-eating coyotes, or helping to bolster a private deer herd's numbers, you will be gaining that much more trust and respect from the landowner.

I like to use lone howls and fawn-in-distress calls while hunting this time of year, which takes place throughout May and June, depending on the species and birthing season. Sometimes regular rabbit or bird distress calls will work, but I have found that coyotes are more interested in spending time with each other and eating fawns than doing their regular hunting at this point in the season.

Moon phases have been written about quite extensively in a lot of the predator hunting literature I have read. Full moons offer a lot of light, allowing animals to hunt more successfully at night. No moon means total darkness and restricted night vision, and the animals will be ready to eat come morning. It has even been said that the moon cycles themselves affect coyote behavior. I am sure on some level they do, as the lunar phases seem to affect all life on earth. But in my experience, what phase the moon is in doesn't matter much when it comes to predator hunting. Hungry or curious or territorial animals will still be that way whether the moon is waxing or waning, and I have never killed a disproportionate number of animals during one phase or the other. That being said, I have noticed that animals are not as anxious coming to the call after a night under the full moon, which makes me think that they are responding more out of curiosity or greed than hunger.

You should always be aware of other hunting seasons that are taking place. In Arizona most of our land is public, so we have to share it. I have had to cancel stands based on ATV riders, deer hunters, and quail hunters. I have had hikers approach my stand, searching for the sound's origin. My point is to be courteous to others who may be using the same areas as you. If you notice big game hunters pursuing animals nearby, give them a wide berth.

Not everyone will do the same for you, but act as if they would. On the same token, be very respectful with your ATV riding – too much of our public lands and roads are being closed off due to irresponsible ATV riders.

      This awareness of other seasons also needs to be seen from a safety point of view. You don't want a very curious deer hunter shooting at the movement in the brush when you're screaming out your dying rabbit woes. I was predator hunting with a friend during the opening week of elk season here in Arizona back in 2008. We thought that we were far enough away from all the hunters, but as we neared the halfway point in our stand a couple of elk hunters, rifles at the ready, came creeping into the clearing we were sitting at the edges of. I silenced the call and the next few moments were a little tense as I waited for them to relax a little before calling out to them. We all got a laugh out of it but it could have turned out not so funny. So just be careful when you're hunting in the vicinity of other people – especially if they have guns!

      Whether you choose to hunt coyotes throughout the year, or choose to hunt them only during certain seasons, it does not matter. Pursue your interests and do not let others easily sway your beliefs. We all hunt different terrain under different circumstances, and it is not logical to think that one system will work for everyone in every situation.

The sun was just starting to show its first light as Scott Francom and I slipped into a stand in the southern deserts of Arizona. It was going to be a full day of hunting for us, and we were anxious to get started.

We set up our ladders in front of some brush and waited for the sun to give us ample shooting light. In this thick brush, we were both armed with shotguns and could see a lot of territory from the perches of our ladders. Scott soon began a morning wake-up call of dying rabbit. Almost as quickly as he began, we both heard sounds behind us and a kit fox came into our stand. Scott saw it first as it circled around him, looking for the call and heading straight in my direction. As he entered my line of sight, he was no more than 10 feet from the base of my ladder, and I hit him with a load of buckshot that sent him screaming underneath a creosote bush, where he quickly expired. I was really excited! Just a little over a minute into our first stand and we already had an animal down.

I didn't have much time to celebrate, though, as a coyote came charging into the area, heading straight for Scott's call. He had come in from the opposite direction, yet still had to have heard the shot – it hadn't even been a full minute since I had fired! I leveled my shotgun on the coyote and fired again, dumping him right where he was. 2 animals down in less than 3 minutes on the first stand of the day - what a fantastic experience.

Maybe the coyote had heard the fox scream, maybe he was coming for the rabbit, but either way, it turned out to be one exciting stand!

1 fox and 1 coyote in less than 3 minutes makes for a good stand

After The Shot

You're out in the field, you do everything just as you should and it all comes together – here comes Wile E. You settle the crosshairs on him and POW! Now that you've finally got an animal to come in, what happens after you pull the trigger? First of all, save the victory dance (or pouting) for some other time. After you shoot, whether you kill an animal or miss it, sit tight and keep calling; multiples on a stand are not uncommon. I've had additional animals come in after a shot, and even had missed animals come back for another round! It may never be known what animals think a gunshot is. Whether they think its thunder on a sometimes cloudless day or simply a loud and abrasive noise, it does not always scare them off. I have even shot at animals that stuck around after a miss, such as a fox that actually looked at the bullet impact to his left before I drilled him with the second shot. There are videos out there on the Internet and in hunting videos that show hunters getting multiple shots at coyotes that stopped a few yards away from each shot opportunity, as if analyzing what just happened. Bobcats usually will not stick around after a missed shot, and are often spooked away by simple out of place noises, but can often be called back given enough time and patience.

Sometimes you'll shoot and swear your shot was true, only to go over there and find no animal and no blood. Your buddy says "See? You missed." How did he know? Well perhaps he knows about 'meat report', or the very pleasing sound a bullet makes when it contacts flesh. It sounds a lot like a WHOP sound, or like the sound that's made when you cup your hands and then try to clap. If it was a close range shot, it's hard to hear the meat report, as your brain is still processing the gunshot. But if it's anything outside of 30 yards you should hear it. Mind you, you won't get this sound when you hit them with a shotgun, but at shotgun ranges, it won't matter.

There is something to be said for missing – everyone does it at one point or another. I've missed predators at 20 feet and I've missed them at 150 yards. We all get 'coyote fever' sometimes and just flat out miss. Don't let it ruin your hunt. Tell yourself that next time you'll be prepared - more patient, more observant, ready to do the opposite of whatever caused you to miss the shot. You'll miss a few animals every now and then, that's just part of an action-packed sport.

Hopefully it will be the exception and not the rule, but you will find yourself trying to track down a wounded animal from time to time. Predators, and all animals, really, are very resilient, and will not die easily unless you score a vital shot. Even then, as mentioned in one of my earlier stories, an animal can run quite a ways on adrenaline alone. Most of the time these solidly hit animals will die quickly and within a short distance, leaving an easy trail for you to follow. It's the hurried or poorly placed shots that will have you chasing an animal into the wild beyond. When I wound an animal, I like to give it a few minutes to run a bit and then lie down and bleed out, which happens more often than not. If that isn't the case, then you need to get down and dirty to find their trail – literally. Go to the last location where you saw them, and start to work in circles around the spot, gradually growing wider until you find blood or hair. Do it again if necessary, and look to new spots where the animal may have run. Pay close attention to grass or brush or anything it may have rubbed up against while moving. Try to think where you might head if you were trying to get away and wounded; this usually means into thicker brush, where the down and dirty part comes in. Try not to walk on tracks or blood spore, and mark locations where you find sign. Don't just focus on the ground – look up and study terrain, as wounded animals generally choose the path of least resistance, including going downhill and through washes. Watch for movement – I've been tracking wounded animals and seen them move up ahead, offering me a finishing shot. If I would've had my nose to the ground, I might not have caught them. Do your absolute best to recover all animals you shoot, as it is your ethical responsibility as a hunter to do so.

Now when you score a solid hit and the animal is down, what next? What you decide to do at this point depends entirely on whether or not you desire to sell or collect pelts. If you want to keep the pelt, then the sooner you get an animal out of its skin, the better. Too much heat and that hide will begin to slip, or in other words, the hair will begin to come out, rendering the pelt useless.

Skinning is a little tougher after the animal has been frozen, but freezing will save you from ticks and flea, which can potentially have diseases.

If it's cold enough outside and the animal is going to stay cool, then that works well, otherwise you either need to skin them out or get them on ice, pronto. I like to carry an ice chest to put animals in, though you don't want to put ice against their skin, as this also ruins pelts. Put them in a plastic bag, and then put enough ice in the cooler to keep the pelt cool. I'm not a fast enough skinner that I want to be skinning multiple animals in the field, as it cuts into my hunting time, so I choose to do my skinning later. Once I get home, I wrap them up nice and tight in a couple of garbage bags and toss them in the chest freezer in my garage – you can guess how much my wife loves to have assorted frozen animals in the freezer. Some guys I hunt with have separate freezers for their animals – if you have the space for this in your garage, I highly recommend it. Freezing animals before skinning also eliminates fleas and ticks, as they die in the cold temperature.

There are various methods of skinning, from the 5 minute tube job, which I call 'the smash and grab', and then there's cutting up the belly or down the back to prepare the hide for a mount or for display. You can keep the feet if you want a display piece, or cut them off to facilitate a quick skinning job for a pelt you plan to sell. Pay close attention to cutting when you get around the face – this is the place where most guys will make mistakes and cut off parts they meant to keep, like ears and noses. Tanning the hide is something I have little experience with, and I send all of my tanning jobs off to tanneries that specialize in doing good quality work, like USA Foxx out of Minnesota.

Selling pelts these days is something you really have to want to do in order to make it worth it. Pelts that are in bad shape, i.e. bullet holes, not furred up, scarred, or have too many nicks from skinning are really not going to fetch a premium at the market. Prices fluctuate depending on season and market, though here in Arizona $20 for a coyote, $40 for a fox, and around $300 for a bobcat seem to be average. Coyotes don't always sell 100%, though, often leaving you with pelts on hand. There are market reports available from multiple sources but I would say the Fur Market Report in the magazine *Predator Xtreme* is probably a great place to start. You can pay a trapper, or someone more knowledgeable about selling pelts, to go to market for you, and this will usually cost you about 20%. Be aware of any fees associated with selling pelts, such as export tags.

I prefer to keep my better pelts to display in my home, or to trade pelts I do not want to local taxidermists or sportsmen. My taxidermist gives me cash for full animals, hide on and guts in – all I have to do is get them on the ground and it's money in my pocket, or credit towards taxidermy work.

So what about the ones I don't want, which are mostly coyotes? Well I leave them where they lay, or often I drag them under a bush or tree. Their bodies go back into the ecosystem and there's one less predator around to harass livestock or eat fawns. Dead coyote bodies really don't seem to bother other coyotes, either. I have called in animals that come in without paying much attention to the dead coyote just a few yards from them that I killed a few days or weeks prior.

So if you don't want to sell them, keep them, or leave them lay, what do you do then? Try to find places that will take the donated carcass. Sometimes a place may want them for research – call your local Game and Fish office and see if they have anything planned for your area. I also have a friend that needs a few bobcat carcasses every year so he can use them as training drags for his lion hounds. Perhaps there is even a local zoo or animal sanctuary that would like the pelt for educational or display purposes. And when I'm hunting a ranch, I generally make an effort to take all carcasses to the rancher, to show him that I'm earning my right to hunt his land.

I also have found a hobby in cleaning the skulls of wildlife, especially predators. I have quite a good collection and it's a fun and even profitable way to do some home taxidermy work. I use colonies of dermestid beetles, which consume all dead organic material, including hair and skin. A colony of these beetles is easy to raise and maintain, though the smell is at times challenging to manage; I have found that the Febreze plug-ins work wonders for this. Once a population gets big, as in a few thousand or more, then cleaning a small skull like a bobcat or fox is an overnight ordeal. After cleaning I prefer to bleach the skulls in 40 Volume peroxide, which can be purchased at any beauty supply store. I let them bleach until they are as white as I'd like them, which generally takes about a week, and then I dry them in the sun for a day or two. Sometimes I will spray them with a clear coat, depending on the look I am after. The clear coat can offer a shiny finish as well as protecting from dust, but I usually prefer the natural dull white appearance. I like to display my skulls, and you'd be surprised how many people who may not be that into hunting are interested in the skulls, as they can see the large, sharp teeth and inner areas of a predator's head, such as the ear canals and brain cavity.

Properly cleaned skulls are great for display – above kit fox (l.) and grey fox (r.)

There are other ways to clean skulls, such as boiling, mastication, and the famous ant hill method. Boiling has been used by many hunters for years, and has produced just as many good looking skulls. The problem is that boiling damages bone. The heat expands the bone, allowing teeth to come loose. Then when the bone cools, the skull shrinks, and can actually turn out smaller than it originally was! Throw in the mess and spousal complaints from the smell, and boiling can be a real hassle.

Mastication is where you place the skull in water and allow the natural bacteria that grow in water to eat the flesh. This is actually a pretty effective method, and requires little work. Simply place the skull in a bucket of water and leave it outside. Depending on the weather, in 2-4 weeks you've got a skull that's ready for bleaching. This method still involves some skull size change, and the teeth will still fall out, but they can be glued back in. The biggest downside to mastication is the smell! I wouldn't recommend doing this unless you've got a couple acres and can always keep the bucket somewhere downwind! If you live in an area that freezes in the winter, then this method will obviously not work during that time.

Using an ant hill is a great idea in theory, but doesn't always work. It can take months to complete, and if you're not always checking the skull or it's not properly secured, then other animals or other people may be tempted to carry off your hard won skull for their own collection. You also have to consider that the sun is brutal to exposed bone, and is prone to cracking it.

And what about eating predators? Are predators a tasty and nutritious food source for humans? Based on that question, I took it upon myself to eat a back strap steak out of a coyote during the winter of 2007. I cooked it without seasoning on my grill, and then ate it. It was not good – tough and chewy dark meat, and the word "gamey" does not begin to describe the urine type tastes I encountered. I documented this whole experience with video and pictures and posted it on a website I often visit called AR15.com. After that coyote, next on the menu was bobcat. Again I ate a back strap steak, un-seasoned and cooked on my grill. Again it was all captured on video. The big difference with bobcat was that it was actually good! Tender, light colored meat, with a pleasant taste and no horrible aroma to purge from the kitchen afterwards. Moral of the story? I wouldn't want to live on coyote meat, but bobcat I sure wouldn't mind, and from what I hear mountain lion makes a fine meal, as well.

After The Shot

No, coyote is not a fine meal (above) – but a tasty bobcat breakfast sure is!

My friend Kelly Lewis is the President and Founder of the Xtreme Predator Callers (XPC) hunting club here in Arizona. There are a number of predator hunting clubs here in Arizona, and every year a few of them get together and organize a multi-club hunt. The multi-club hunt is always hosted by the winner of the previous year's competition, which is based on number of animals killed and certain point values assigned to each species. For the multi-club hunt of 2008 I joined Kelly and his nephew Luke to hunt for the glory of XPC.

We headed to the southwest region of Arizona on a Friday night and camped out, arising early the next morning to begin our hunt. We had a couple of dry stands, and alternated calling responsibility between the three of us, as is common when hunting with partners. It was my turn to call and I chose a stand out in the flats that was covered in creosote bushes, giving coyotes ample safe coverage to approach from. Kelly was to my left and Luke to my right as I began my set. 15 minutes passed with no response and so I signaled to my partners that I was done. As I slowly stood up I saw a coyote circling from behind me, headed toward Kelly's position. The coyote had not seen me, and I decided to take a shot as Kelly was now to my far right and well outside of my firing zone. I shouldered my rifle and as the coyote trotted into an opening I fired. I heard the sound of a solid hit and watched the coyote stumble, yet recover and take off running. I yelled to Kelly "he's headed right to you!" The coyote passed closely by Kelly but he was unable to get a shot off due to the thick cover and fast rate of speed of the dog. I jogged over to Kelly and he said "that coyote's got a hole in his side, he's hit for sure." It was then that we both looked in the direction of travel the coyote had taken, right into even thicker and taller brush cover.

After waiting a few minutes, hoping that the coyote would lie down and die, we hurried towards the coyote's last seen location and spotted a blood trail leading into the thick cover. We began to follow his blood trail, spotting areas where the coyote had laid down and then gotten up as we approached. We worked hard to spot drops of blood and follow blades of grass that had been brushed up against, leaving bloody streaks. The three of us split up, Kelly and I in the brush looking for the coyote, and Luke up on a small rise nearby trying to spot the coyote if he left the brush. Kelly and I wound around and around in the thick vegetation, at times losing the trail and having to go back, and even crawling around on hands and knees trying to locate more blood. The whole time we could only think of being in such close quarters and coming upon a wounded coyote. 35 minutes had passed and we began to worry that the blood would clot from all the dirt the coyote was picking up each time it laid down. We were nearing the end of the brush, which lead to the highway, and were now more than 300 yards away from where we had entered in our search. Luke hadn't seen the coyote leave, so we knew we were getting close.

Kelly decided to step out of the brush to take a look around while I continued to hunt the blood trail. A few minutes had passed when I heard Kelly fire his rifle and say "I got him!" As he had stepped out, he had seen the coyote leave the end of the brush and start to weeble-wobble its way across the flats. It had nearly bled out and could barely stand as Kelly fired the finishing shot, putting an end to a long tracking job. I had hit the coyote in the ribs, not holding far enough in front of him as he trotted. The wound had left a large exit but had missed the vitals and allowed the coyote to continue to operate despite his bleeding wound.

I felt a little badly about the poor shot as I looked the coyote over, and we all discussed what a long tracking job that had been – it took us 40 minutes to finish the job. We were hunting in a competition, so it was very important that we recover all possible animals, but I would like to think that had we not been competing we would have still dedicated the same amount of time to finding the wounded coyote, who clearly was a worthy adversary.

After our hard tracking job, we still had a decent contribution to the club lineup.

Competitions

Two old predator callers were sitting around the campfire after a full day of hunting. One leaned closer to the fire and said "I sure have killed a lot of coyotes in my time". The other raised his hat and said "That's true, but not as many as I have". Then the first one extends his hand and says "Wanna bet?" Thus was born the predator calling competition.

Whether for profit, fame, or friendship, predator calling competitions have been around for a long time. The most popular is the World Calling Contest, referred to as simply the Worlds. The entry fee is high and so are the stakes, for it's not just money and prizes that await the winners, it's the recognition. Just ask Al Morris and Garvin Young, who are the only team to win back-to-back titles, and who currently are the only team to hold three total titles, including being the current defending champions. This is quite the feat, seeing as how they compete against well over a hundred other teams.

You don't have to hunt the Worlds to hunt in a competition environment, however. There are probably many local competitions in your area, including hunts put on by predator hunting clubs and those put on by passionate predator callers, working outside of club rules. If competition style hunting is your thing, then you should be able to find one within driving distance of your house.

Competitions have helped our sport by raising awareness of the excitement and fulfillment of participating in predator hunting. They bring friends and often family together for a fun event that allows for our natural competitiveness as humans to be brought out in our favorite sport. Vendors, calling gear manufacturers, local economies where the competition is held, and of course the winners all benefit from these events.

Ready For Anything

A typical line-up for a one day club competition

If you decide to participate in a competition, there are a few important factors that will help you. First and foremost, scout the terrain! Get a map of the area, talk to anybody that may know where the predators are hanging out, scout every possible good stand, and then mark them numerically so that you can hunt them in a time-efficient manner. Make sure that you know where the boundaries are, and where the check-in location is – don't be late! Second, stick to the time standard for calling a stand, which is 15 minutes, and don't spend time debating new stand locations that are not on the map. Third, pack lots of high energy snacks, water, and any tools you may need to fix your vehicle. You should be carrying all of that anyways, but it is especially important here, where time is of the essence. Fourth, pick a good partner; nearly all competitions consist of team hunting and you don't want a partner that is going to ruin your stands or get tired before the end of the day. Fifth, last, and most important – have fun! Enjoy the spirit of competition and play to win.

    I have hunted in quite a few competitions, both for prizes and for recognition. Sometimes I come out on top, sometimes I don't, but I always enjoy the company of good friends and fellow hunters. That being said, I do not prefer competitions. Anytime you offer money as a reward for doing something well, there will be those with the desire to cheat. Try as they may, the clubs and organizers of these competitions just can't catch them all. There are a number of ways to perform dishonorably in a calling competition, none of which I will describe here, but suffice it to say that not all of them can be easily detected.

    Competitions, while fun, also present an element I prefer to keep out of calling – the feeling of work. When I am scouting new area, hiking the hills while heading to a stand, or sitting in the Arizona sun awaiting the arrival of Wile E., I am definitely sweating; but it is the sweat of enjoyment, not of labor. Often when I hunt competitions there is a rushed feeling – heading quickly from one stand to another, avoiding unnecessary conversation, eating meals rapidly to avoid wasting time. Then there are those who end up wanting, and in their 'shame' don't even show up to the check-in, preferring to go home rather than showing up empty handed. Whether my count is thin or flush I really enjoy going to check-in, as there is such a long line of dead predators, and guys and gals are there with congratulations and stories of missed opportunities. Sometimes you'll get to see a three legged coyote, or a mountain lion, or a one-eyed bobcat. Yet the spirit of fierce competition keeps too many away, and prevents others from even trying. That is why I do not prefer competitions; though you will still find me hunting in one occasionally – but it is usually for the pleasure of the hunt, and the great company of my fellow hunters.

After a long and exhausting day of work there are few things more satisfying for me than to spend some time on a stand, hunting my favorite animal - the coyote. After one such day of work I found myself driving to one of my favorite hunting spots that is both close to my home and filled with coyotes.

After parking my truck near the road I hiked about a ½ mile into the area, crossing a few washes and climbing up a few hills. I approached a hill top that gave me a great view of the valley below me, and was covered with good thick brush in which to conceal myself. With the sun to the west and quickly descending to the horizon, I chose a spot on the hilltop that offered me a view of everything below the hill, except for a few yards at the base which were covered in thick scrub oak.

I nestled into the stand, sitting as far back into the brush as I could. To my rear was a host of thick bushes and cacti – the wind was blowing across my left side and I felt as if the setup couldn't be better. With this in mind, I began my calling sequence.

I was about 3 or 4 minutes into the set when I first spotted the coyote, trotting in from 300 yards out. There were no obstacles between him and my location, so I stopped calling and just watched his approach. I get a lot of satisfaction out of watching predators in the wild, learning their mannerisms and observing their movements.

When he broke the 100 yard line I lip squeaked to keep him on track. With renewed vigor he picked up his pace and entered the brush at the base of the hill. I used this time to begin to raise my rifle in expectation that when he exited the brush I would take the shot. I waited and waited – no coyote. Was this coyote Houdini? Where could he have possibly gone? Did he catch my rifle movement and is now hung up in the brush? I lip squeaked some more, hoping to entice him in. 3 minutes passed and no sign of the coyote. I began to think all was lost, that my coyote had simply vanished.

I was suddenly aware of noise in the brush behind me. Always concerned about a cougar getting the drop on me, I turned my head and was nearly nose to nose with my long lost coyote! His eyes about popped out of head as he kicked it sideways to get away, tripping himself up in the brush and nearly falling down. I yelled out in surprise and fell over on my side, trying to get my rifle around for a shot. He ran Hell bent for the edge of the hill, dropping over the side and onto the valley floor just as I brought my rifle to bear. I stood up as quickly as possible and caught sight of him as he raced for the brush line, already nearly 100 yards away. I raised my rifle and caught him in the scope, but started to laugh and dropped my rifle to my side, watching as the coyote ran like a freight train to get to safety.

If you would have asked me right then, I would have said that coyote was 100 pounds with red eyes and 6 inch canines and that he stood 4 foot at the shoulder. Once I was able to collect myself and check my shorts, things came into perspective and I realized he was actually a pretty small dog - probably his first year out of the den. I figure that when he entered the brush at the base of the hill, he turned east while hidden inside of it and followed it around the base until he got behind me, trying to get downwind. He entered the brush hoping to surprise a rabbit but surprised another hunter instead!

I laugh about it now because really we were just two young guys, both trying to have a good afternoon and both getting the surprise of our lives!

Where's Rizzo?

I frequently post in the Small Game and Trapping forum on the website AR15.com, where I go by the screen name of "rizzo1318". A lot of hunters that are new to predator calling often ask about camouflage selection. My answers are generally the same, so one day I decided to take my son, a camera, and a few different camo clothing sets out to some of my hunting terrain and do a little photo work. My son and I were mostly just having fun, but after I posted the information in the forum, I got a lot of positive remarks on the camo tests. Based on those responses I decided to include the same information in this book.

Camo is a widely debated thing in predator hunting. I've seen it all and worn most of it, and these days, I just stick to the basics. But after a stand and around the campfire, I've heard every angle: "Ghillie's are best!" or "It doesn't matter what pattern, as long as you sit still" or my favorite "I don't even wear camo, just jeans and a worn-out shirt". And it's a question every hunter seems to have asked at least once, so here's some pictures mixed in with my opinions and experience.

Let's sum it up, because everyone has their own personal taste. First, match your surroundings as far as color is concerned. Second, intricate camo patterns are made to please your eyes, not the animals. At a distance, that cool little leaf / twig / bug pattern is just a colored blob. Third, wash it before you wear it, wear it before you hunt in it. And finally, break up that outline - the ultimate stand killer is the dreaded "head-neck" combo that screams "I'm a human!" Then keep the sun to your back, stop scratching yourself and sit still!

Here are some pictures of some guys I hunt with. Out of 6 different guys, you'll see a few of the same camo types, but each guy has a different configuration and a different color set. Even walking to a stand, some of these guys are already blending in.

Now we'll take a look at a few of my "camo tests". First of all I have to thank my skilled and experienced photographer, who also happens to be my 5-year-old son, Garret.

One of the first mistakes I see guys make is not covering up their face and hands. These parts shine like a Nashville Star, and even the most basic face mask and gloves help. Here's a setup where I compare mask to no mask - you can easily see my face without the mask. Get a little closer and let the sun shine off of it, and a face really gives away your position.

Ready For Anything

So what about camo color and stand selection? Use the colors that match your surroundings, of course, but the argument of light vs. dark colors is void when you choose stands that allow you to sit in the shade and get in close to brush, where either color will break up your outline. Here's me in some light desert camo, sitting in the sun vs. sitting in the shade.

    In each picture my camo blends, but in the shade my outline is broken up much easier. Even with darker colors, choosing a stand that allows you to sit farther back in to the brush and take advantage of the sun will pay dividends when an animal is searching for you.

    In the following set of pictures, you'll be able to see where in the shade I can even get away with putting my rifle on a bipod and having it ready for the shot, whereas out in the open, every extra outline and every movement is more easily seen. The sun often reflects off of any available surface, and that reflection can be seen from a long ways away.

Where's Rizzo?

Now to the topic of the ghillie suit. I have heard it all considering this topic. A lot of guys think it's overkill, that it's too "tactical" or too "military". I've got to admit, when I'm out there in my BDUs and my ghillie with my AR-15 slung across my back, I'm sure it may look a little odd, but it doesn't matter - no one can see me!

Seriously though, a ghillie is the best way to break up your outline. No regular camo can come close. And by ghillie, I mean a standard jute or burlap setup, 3D leafy camo or whatever it is that you have that has material hanging from it. Ghillie suits literally make your outline disappear. Such a suit allows smaller movements, like getting you rifle into position or manipulating calls, to go unseen. A few weeks ago, after a stand was over, I stood up in my ghillie and looked behind me to see a coyote circling around to my downwind. There I was, standing straight up, 50 yards from this dog, and when he looked at me, his eyes just kept going - his body language didn't change at all. I don't think he even saw me as I raised my rifle and then dropped the hammer on him. So there's the upsides but what about the downsides? Well, a regular ghillie can really warm you up - I don't even think about mine during the summer months. It gets caught on some bushes, but it's no big deal - it gets uncaught just as fast and has never compromised my safety or anything like that. Price is also a factor - most ghillies or 3D camo is not cheap, but it's worth it. And where the 3D camo really has the advantage is in its construction. As an example, a friend of mine has a full suit that is mesh construction, meaning that he can wear shorts and a t-shirt in the summer, throw the suit over himself, be fully covered and yet the mesh allows for good air circulation. Now it's still hot to wear, but in the same conditions, my jute ghillie is almost deadly hot. During most of the spring, and all of the fall and winter, my ghillie is an excellent tool for helping me to hide. How excellent? Take a look at the following pictures. Same stand, same time of day - first with regular camo, then with ghillie added. First picture the sun was even behind the clouds, which helped.

Where's Rizzo?

I only utilize a ghillie jacket, with short sleeves, so as to not get tangled with my rifle or calls. Pants would help, but as you can see in the next few pictures, even just a jacket can help you become just another part of the landscape.

And now it's time for: Where's Rizzo?

Where's Rizzo?

In the last picture, you can see why standing is one of my favorite ways to kill predators while among the trees. It allows your body to fully conceal itself using all of your camo options, and it gives you greater range of motion while putting your head and rifle above the heads of your prey. Plus, you can just see more terrain.

Now we'll take a look at equipment. Your #1 piece of equipment and the only thing you really need to have on stand other than some calls is your firearm. Regardless of your firearm choice, it needs to be able to blend in as well as you do. Most everyone I talk to says "most rifles and shotguns have wood stocks, and wood is brown like nature, so it'll blend without help". Well, just like camo patterns, firearms are made to appeal to the buyer, not the animals. That wooden Monte Carlo stock with the all-weather lacquer finish looks really great in the store or in your gun safe, but how about in the outdoors? Let's examine how one of my stock rifles (with above mentioned stock) looks in the brush, especially when it's getting hit by a little sun.

See what I mean? Not only does it shine, but its outline really stands out. It may be brown, but it's a hard object, it doesn't flow into the surroundings like you all dressed in your camo would. A little matte camo wrap or some paint would go a long way, and during my big game hunts, that rifle gets a good dose of camo wrap. Did you see my camo painted AR in the same picture?

So now that we've seen some various camo, just how much is all this going cost? Do I really need all this crap? The answer is: Not much and not necessarily. I have a friend who's camo consists of a lightweight natural tones mesh poncho, a green cap and some cheap camo pants. You might have noticed him in the first set of pictures. Now that guy can blend in anywhere, and there are times when I've looked over him while scanning terrain. He still wears camo gloves and a camo face mask, along with the hood from his poncho to break up the "head-neck" outline I talked about earlier. Good natural tones and a little camo go a long way. Remember what Garret was wearing? Some cheap camo pants and a green jacket. Add a face mask and a camo hat and *Voila!* He's gone.

So just how much do I spend on all that camo? Everything I wear is basic, inexpensive stuff. I started out calling predators wearing my Army woodland BDUs and at times I still wear them. Mostly for darks I wear MARPAT BDUs, which work great and take a beating, and you can get a full set for about $80. For my lights I wear some Sage Country shirts ($20), some of those Wal-Mart desert camo shirts ($10), and some Vanish pants ($40). Gloves and face masks I usually buy on clearance at Bass Pro or Sportsman's Warehouse for $5 or $10 bucks each. Camo caps are a dime a dozen, and easy to come by - a lot of companies put their name on a camo cap for advertising, and some even pass them out for free. Boonie hats, which can be had for about $15, are also a great way to help that outline breakup, plus during the summer months they really keep that sun off of your neck and ears. As for my ghillie, it can be had from Rancho Safari for about $70, with full suits getting around $150. 3D camo runs about the same in price, with the Scent-Lok suits reaching into the $200 range. If you don't want a ghillie suit of any kind, I highly recommend always paying attention to how your head and neck are looking - I see guys get all situated on stand, with their body behind cover and that head of theirs sticking up or out, looking around and getting seen. You can also get a good face mask and hat combo, or get a stand-alone ghillie hood, which is ideal.

  My point to all of this is to take what you have and see how it works. Don't go out and find the absolute best spot where your camo is guaranteed to blend in, take a picture, look at it and say "Wow! I can't even see myself!" Leave that hocus-pocus advertising to the camo manufacturers. When I am checking my camo, I do just what I did for the above pictures. I go to my normal stand terrain, pick stands, and take some pictures. Then I can see what stands are good choices, and which ones aren't. Doing this little photo-shoot, I found some camo setups that were downright horrible. Another good resource is the people you hunt with. I ask my buddies how well I blend in, and they ask me the same. Garret is a great observer, as well, though he's a little biased towards my abilities.

    Well I hope this demonstration was able to explain some of the basics of camo. I'm sure there is someone out there who is going to totally disagree with me, and that's fine. Remember, this is all just my experience mixed in with some Rizzo Philosophy.

The Future Of Our Sport

I mentioned before that I don't like statistics – they're all politically driven, one way or the other. I hear some say there are plenty of new hunters coming into the sport, and I hear others say that hunters are a dying breed. I guess I agree with both sides. You see, I'm a Boy Scout leader and I know how many of my young Scouts are hunters – one. One single Scout is a hunter, out of the twelve in our Troop. So what about the others? Well that's up to us. You see, with video games and TV and all the other "cool" things to do, being in the outdoors just doesn't sound like fun to some of these kids. Until you take them shooting, or fishing, or small game hunting. You have to introduce as many kids into the outdoors as possible to ensure there is some interest left, even if it's just a tiny seed of knowledge that they have. That seed may bud later into a passion for the outdoors, or may live forever as simple knowledge. But it will affect how they vote, and how they act, and how they feel about wildlife and habitat preservation. I have made sure that all of my own kids are introduced to the outdoors at a young age, and lucky for me, they love it.

My friend and fellow predator hunting enthusiast Jason LeMarr feels the same way I do. After bringing his son, Rhett, onto stand with him a number of times, Jason decided to put a rifle in the boy's hands - and what a story that turned out to be.

The day that my oldest, Rhett, was born, I called him my Lil' Man. I will tell you that your kids will grow fast - I know mine have. As Rhett grew, he toted camouflage clothes around the house, carried toy guns and even shot the TV with a toy bow that shoots foam balls. He then proceeded to say, "The elk is down; I got him, Dad!" It was hard to scold him for shooting the TV. My son shot his first elk, and it was just funny to watch him.

Rhett kept growing as the years went by, never slowing down at all. He has often seen me bring coyotes home after a morning of calling. Mom would bundle him up and out the door he came with excitement to see what Dad had. He was full of questions of what happened and how it happened. His interest made me excited, thinking that we could be calling partners someday. After he got the answers to the questions, he wanted to get pictures taken with the coyotes. As Rhett got older, he became my main photographer. In fact, Rhett took a lot of the pictures on my website, beginning at the age of 4.

    When Rhett was just 5 and 6, I let him tag along a few times while I was calling coyotes. The more he went and the more videos we watched, coupled with the schooling from me, the more educated he became. At 5 years old, if he were asked, "What do you do to get a coyote to stop for the shot?" He would reply confidently, "Bark at him." Or if asked, "What do you do if you see a coyote first and Dad doesn't?" He would lip squeak. The mold was about set, and the time was getting closer for him.

    One day when Rhett was 6 years old, he and I went to a good friend's property to call coyotes. I told him that it was very important that he not wiggle around and that he do the right thing because I was 99.9% confident that we would call a coyote at this location. He replied, "I'm on it, Dad." We got situated. I had Rhett looking over one section, and I looked the other. I reminded him with the question, "You know what to do if you see one?" He nodded his head. I began calling on the "Tweaked Squirrel" to manipulate the dinner bell for the coyotes. Rhett was almost motionless. I whispered to him, "You are doing awesome." Ten minutes had elapsed and I had this overwhelming feeling to keep looking over my shoulder. I kept a lookout behind us and at the 20-minute mark of the stand I threw out a couple of non-dominant howls with my "Hi-Jacker" open reed call. We sat there for a few minutes without a sound. I looked a few more times over my shoulder at the back door and nothing was there. I looked at Rhett and observed him as he was there watching the section I gave him. I was as proud as I could be of him. A couple of minutes had passed since I howled on the "Hi-Jacker". I slowly eased my head back to check behind us. Wouldn't you know it? A pair of coyotes was at our back door. The wind and decoy should have had them exposing themselves in front of us. I quietly whispered to Rhett, "We've got two coyotes behind us. Slowly turn around." He slowly turned to see and I asked, "Do you see them yet?" Rhett responded in a crackling voice, "Yes." I told Rhett that when the lead coyote turns his head back at the other one, I would swing around and get on him. The lead coyote turned his head; I turned around on him and he was in my scope. Unfortunately, a post was between the coyote and me. Now I anxiously looked at the rear coyote. The rear coyote must not have noticed the movement; his behavior seemed comfortable. I looked back through the scope, thinking to myself, "It doesn't get any better." Rhett was getting to see all this unfold before his eyes. I then noticed the lead coyote I had in my scope turning around and beginning to trot away at approximately 100 yards. As I got ready to bark at the coyote, Rhett let out a loud bark, the coyote stopped and I let the Rock River AR-15 send a 60 grain Hornady V-Max at the coyote. Crack! The coyote was hit. I looked at Rhett and smiled, telling him that I wasn't completely ready but ready enough. I was proud of him for knowing what to do. I made sure that he knew that his action was a huge part in the success of that hunt.

One day a few weeks later Rhett told me while I was reloading, "Dad, I think I am ready for my own coyote rifle now." I thought that was priceless and showed him my complete attention and took him seriously. My mind started turning and a month later Rhett had his own rifle. I got him an H & R Youth .223 and topped it with a 3x9x40 scope and a Harris bipod. You should have seen his expression when he saw it. The first thing he asked was, "Can we go shoot it?" I told him, "Not until we go over safety, the dos and don'ts, cleaning and handling." Rhett has a good understanding of safety. He has been drilled about safety with his BB gun and bow enough from me; it should be imbedded in his mind. However, every time we take out the gun or bow, I always remind him of the rules.

We went out to our Uncle Melvin's; he has a 100, 200 and 300 yard range at his house. I got Rhett's rifle sighted in and *proceeded to teach and work with him on everything from beginning to end of each shot. Rhett began to hit paper at 100 yards with groups that would hammer a coyote. I was impressed at this point. The next few months we worked on his shooting, and with each trip out to Uncle Melvin's, he was improving.*

It came time that Rhett was to make his first stand with rifle in hand. I went over all aspects with him on the dos, don'ts and safety. I was confident that he comprehended everything, and we were ready to walk to our first stand together. I told Rhett on the way out that I would be the back-up gunner and that he would get the first shot if a coyote came in. I also told him not to get upset if he missed as I have missed many coyotes myself.

As we approached our stand, I looked down at Rhett. I could see that this was a big day for him. I got him situated and pointed in the right direction. The decoy was set, and I nestled in. I asked, "Rhett, are you ready?" He nodded his head, and you could see from the smile under his facemask that he was excited.

I started calling this stand with the FoxPro FX5 and the Jack-in-the-Box decoy. I watched Rhett as the distress sounds were being played; he was scanning slowly just as if he had done this many times before. Ten minutes into calling, Rhett's legs and feet went to sleep. He was really uncomfortable and upset, thinking it would end the stand. I told Rhett to get on his knees and I would lengthen the Harris bi-pod to the correct height. He was now back in the game and ready to proceed. I whispered to Rhett that I was going to howl and not to jump. He jumped anyway. At the fifteen-minute mark in the stand, I let out two non-dominant howls with the "Hi-Jacker." After the howls, I told Rhett to keep a close eye on anything that might come into view.

A couple of minutes went by and out in the wide open a coyote came trotting in. I said to Rhett, "Hey, look out in front of you – a coyote." He got behind his scope and said to me, while the coyote is 200 yards out, "I'm on him, want me to take him?" I replied to Rhett, "No, the coyote is unalarmed and comfortable. We have the sun at our back and he can't see us." When the approaching coyote closed in at 150 yards Rhett asked, "Do I take him now?" Once again I told him not to shoot. I said, *"Relax and stay calm. I will let you know."* At this point it really got exciting for me. It was time to tell my son to take his first shot at a coyote. The coyote was now at 100 yards and I needed to do something before the coyote got downwind. I told Rhett, *"Get your cross-hairs on him. I will bark to get him to stop and when I do, make a good shot."* Rhett said, *"I'm on him."* I proceeded to bark at the coyote. The third time I barked, the coyote stopped and Rhett dropped the hammer on his H & R Youth .223. The coyote was hit hard and tried to get away. I knew if I didn't pull up on him, the coyote would enter a patch of standing corn. If he did, we could lose him, so I hit him again with my .204 Ruger CZ 527. The coyote dropped. Rhett excitedly said, "Dad, he's down, I seen it in my scope, he's down!" I looked at Rhett and told him how proud I was. We tried to keep calling, but I was as excited as Rhett and called it quits. We went to get Rhett's first coyote. When I walked up on the coyote, and said here it is, Rhett let out an excited war whoop. I hooked the coyote to the drag, got some pictures, and asked Rhett what he thought. As we were trekking back 500 yards to the truck, Rhett was so excited he talked a mile a minute the whole time. It was awesome for him and it was awesome for me. I will never forget this moment, neither will Rhett.

My challenge to each and every hunter is; introduce someone to the outdoors. It is a rewarding feeling and it ensures that our great hunting heritage will last.

Through Jason's hard work and patience, his son has learned to love the outdoors, and also to enjoy coyote hunting. I'm sure that as his daughter grows she, too, will play an active part in the outdoors. Not all kids are going to enjoy shooting, or fishing, or sitting still for 15 minutes on a coyote stand, but that doesn't mean we can't introduce them to every aspect of the sportsman's way of life. Make sure that you don't force something onto a young person – give them time and they will find their passion. Not everyone can be a great fisherman or a great hunter, but everyone can learn to appreciate the beautiful and bounteous world God has given us.

    The shooting sports, hiking, camping, and fishing are activities that will assist our kids in improving their self-esteem and their confidence. I have watched boys who participate in Boy Scouts go from pre-teen kids unsure of their place in the world to positive and dependable young men who feel as if no obstacle is too tall to overcome. They have gained this sure mind and spirit through positive and challenging experiences while participating in many outdoor activities.

    My own children are so sure of themselves in the outdoors that you would never guess their age while observing their abilities. I smile every time that my son spots deer on a far off hill or my oldest daughter walks to the water's edge to observe the creatures swimming there. My youngest daughter is too small to be on her own yet, but already she is happier and more excited when we are outdoors.

    So the next time you head to a stand, the range, or your favorite fishing hole, remember to take a kid with you – our future depends on it.

Ready For Anything

Closing Advice

A lot of people learn about calling but very few get serious about it. Here's why: sitting still for 20 minutes at a time, shutting their mouths when it's go time, they don't practice with their firearms and so they can't hit anything, it's too hot, it's too cold, the ground is too hard, and the most common "where are the animals?" You can call for 8 stands and have nothing show up and then the next 4 stands will produce. You may call 12 animals in one day and then the very next day call 1. You see where I'm going with this? Patience is a virtue when you are calling.

Check out a couple of predator hunting videos by knowledgeable and informative guys, like Randy Anderson. There are a lot of BANG-FLOP videos out on the market, as well as on the web, but watching coyotes get shot, while entertaining, is not educational. Read up in hunting magazines, like *Predator Xtreme*, and check out websites like PredatorMasters.com, PredatorProfessionals.com, or the Outdoors Forums of AR15.com. There are sure to be some predator hunting or trapping clubs in your area – check one out, as they often offer novice hunts. Here in Arizona I have always enjoyed the company of the members from 'Xtreme Predator Callers' and also 'Arizona Predator Callers'. Once you get all fired up, get out there and experiment. Your first few times may be rough, and one animal in every 10 stands is probably a good scale, it may be even 1 in every 15 for a while. It might be more – it may take you weeks to get the hang of it, but once you do, you won't regret the effort it took to get there. The successful predator hunters are the guys who stick with it and keep hunting. I have been hunting with actual professionals and got one animal in 20 stands, then gone out the next day and killed 6 in a couple of hours. So don't get discouraged - calling is an adventure and the more time you spend at it, the better you'll get. Remember, the guys in the videos don't show the stands where nothing comes in, and they rarely show when they miss. It's something that happens so you might as well get used to it, just don't get discouraged by it.

Your success will vary from other hunters, but be careful when using the word "success". Everyone may have a different measure of "hunting success" - I know I do. When I get to go out and enjoy the world and the abilities God blessed me with, then I am successful, even without fur on the ground. Just enjoy the adventure, and your "success" will come in its own time.

And remember, above all, be ***ready for anything!***

Other Methods Of Take

Billy Stilson with a black bear near Jackson Hole, Wyoming, taken sometime in the early 1950s.

Game and Fish departments for every state in the U.S. have the responsibility to list every legal or illegal way to take, or kill, game animals. But there are a few ways that don't totally fall into one classification or the other. These are categorized as "other methods of take".

My family members have been involved in hunting for many generations, for sport and relaxation and as a means to make a living. I felt that no good hunting book would be complete without some family stories about the good ol' days. Stories from the era when not every place on the map had been explored, and when "other methods of take" were often used!

The Stilsons helped to settle the Jackson Hole, Wyoming territory. My great-grandfather was a trapper and bear hunter, a real predator killer who hunted grizzlies in the backcountry. You can read about one of his adventures in the January 1959 issue of Outdoor Life, an article entitled "Cold Storage Grizzlies", penned by Bill Stilson. He and his three sons owned and operated Crystal Creek Outfitters, a big game hunting and guiding business. They would take people from all over the world deep into the Wyoming Wilderness on horseback in pursuit of big game. Needless to say, my predecessors were true mountain men who roamed the wilds and used the land properly, showing proper respect to the circle of life. That is, until the introduction of snowmobiles . . . .

My grandfather, Glen Stilson, for whom I was named, was a man who loved a good time and a good joke. He and his friend Evart would often ride snowmobiles across Antelope Flats, a once free and open country nestled beneath the Teton Mountains. As they sped across the open snow tundra, they would spot coyotes and head right for them. It didn't take coyotes long to tire of being chased by snowmobiles, so they would wait until the snowmobile was almost upon them and then jump to the side. Once the snowmobile passed, they would jump onto the now beaten down snow left by the machine and head the other direction, effectively giving my grandfather and his friend the slip. This became pretty common operating procedure until one day, when my grandfather was in his early 40's.

Glen Lacey Stilson, late 1950s

He was speeding across the snow after a coyote, and as the coyote leapt to the side, perhaps out of reflex, Glen reached out and flipped that coyote's tail. This caused the coyote to tumble around in the snow in a cartwheel type fashion until being able to right itself and heading off in the other direction as usual. Well Evart thought this was the funniest thing he'd ever seen, and he set about to do it himself. This became a game known as "Tailing Coyotes". They didn't really ever get another one, but after a ride they would sit around and talk about how close they came to doing it. Little did Evart know that his time would soon come.

One beautiful winter day, as the morning ride commenced, Evart spotted a coyote out on the tundra. He ripped his throttle wide open and gave chase. Quickly catching up to the coyote, he reached his hand out, expecting the coyote to leap out of reach.

But instead, he grabbed a handful of coyote tail! He flipped the tail forward as fast as he could, but the coyote had other ideas and kicked to the left, landing squarely on the seat in front of Evart! The coyote looked back at Evart as they sped across the tundra, but Evart was already making his escape as he pushed himself off of the back of the sled. He then watched as the coyote sat tight and rode the snowmobile another 50 yards before it came to a stop, then the coyote jumped off and ran into the forest.

When Glen got to his friend Evart, he asked "Why did you jump off?" to which Evart replied "I guess it was his turn to drive!"

'Alley Oop' was a caveman and the title character in a comic strip of the same name that was started back in 1932. Alley Oop was a big strong brute who would have rather fought dinosaurs than deal with his fellow cavemen. It was no surprise, then, that my Dad's cousin and fellow wild man David earned this nickname in school.

David was a very big guy who spent a lot of his free time in the mountains, often running trap lines. It was on one such trip that David was nearing the end of his trap line when he encountered a coyote that was not properly hung up in the trap. He was loading his last .22 round into his rifle when the coyote broke free; David shot at it as it ran, but missed. As the coyote plunged into the snow covered wilderness it landed in a deep snow bank, and was fumbling around trying to get out when David caught up to it after using his snowshoes to cover the distance rapidly. He immediately jumped on the coyote, which only sank deeper into the snow. He tried to use his rifle butt to hit the coyote in the head, but that just sank them both deeper as well. Out of options and nearing the end of his time in a snowy hole with a desperate coyote, David could think of nothing else than to grab the coyote by the neck, pull it out of the hole, and punch it square in the head. This maneuver did the trick, and the coyote was out cold for good. When he returned home, he went inside to wash his hands after skinning out *the animals from his trap line. It was at this time he realized he was unable to get his high school ring off of his hand. He went to his mother for help, who asked him what had happened to his hand. Not a man for bragging, he replied in a quiet manner "I had to hit a coyote in the head." She then had to get out the pliers to bend and pull the ring off of David's hand, so great was the force with which he hit that coyote*

Robert "Dude" Harrington with a bull elk that he killed in Colorado during November of 1957

My Mom grew up in the 1950's and 60's on a sheep ranch in New Mexico near the ranching community of Picacho. They struggled more with rattlesnakes than with coyotes, but their friends over in Dunlap, the Shirleys, were literally overrun with them. Once a month my Mom, her two sisters, and her father,

Robert "Dude" Harrington, would make the two and a half hour drive to Dunlap. They went to help with the cattle, but during the early morning hours they helped out with something else – coyotes. Coyotes ravaged their cattle herds, and it was a serious necessity to thin them out.

Prentice and Gladys Shirley kept four greyhound dogs on the ranch. Not as pets, but as coyote chasers. They would load up early in the morning, with Dude, Prentice, and two of the Harrington girls in the cab and the dogs in the back of the truck. Using spotlights they would drive the ranch until they spotted a coyote. Dude, who was often driving, would pound on the side of the truck and the dogs would bail out and go to work. The greyhounds would expertly chase down the coyotes, and one of them would bite the coyote by the throat, while the others clamped down on the legs. Sometimes they would kill the coyote before Dude and Prentice could get to them, but often one of the men would have to shoot the coyote.

They would do this until the sun came up, and then it was time to get back to working the cattle. But every morning, for 5 straight days every month, they would hunt coyotes with those greyhounds. They skinned them out and hung the pelts on the fence along the highway. My Mom says she remembers that the pelts seemed to go on for a mile. It was like this at a lot of the ranches in the area, where coyote hunting was a required part of daily living. These days some people may call their methods cruel; but my Mom says that if you've ever seen a pack of coyotes take down a calf, then you'd consider the greyhound technique an act of mercy.

Today, hunters continue to use dogs to help eliminate coyotes. With the growth of animal activist organizations, however, the type of dogs that were described in the previous story are not very commonly used anymore, if ever.

These days I have seen coyote dogs that basically work as living bait. They travel from the stand location out to where coyotes have already been spotted either coming to a call or located with spotting scopes or binoculars. They then entice the coyote to come close enough to be shot by the hunter. "Dogging" is another exciting way to hunt coyotes, and often times the dog you already own can be trained to do this. There are special coyote dogs that can be purchased or trained, though they usually come with a hefty price tag, usually in the range of several thousand dollars. These dogs can also run coyotes down to their den locations or into an inescapable area where they await the arrival of the hunter to kill the coyote. This is a type of coyote hunting that I have seen but never participated in, so I can't give very detailed information about it. I thought it was worth mentioning in this book, however, in case you want to pursue it further.

Product Recommendations

Here is a list of some of the brands I use and like, without endorsement or compensation (dang it).

Except for one:
LeMarr Game Calls (www.lemarrgamecalls.com)
I am a Pro Staff member for LeMarr Game Calls, but I was using his calls before I was ever on his staff. Jason LeMarr is one of the nicest guys you'll ever deal with. He makes beautiful calls, and is very attentive to detail. His reeds and sounds are unique to his calls; which makes them very productive on stand. I highly recommend his "Hi-Jacker" open-reed call, which is the most versatile hand call I have ever used.

Kannah Creek Calls (kannahcreekcalls@yahoo.com)
Mark McCray is a craftsman in every sense of the word. The calls he makes are so unique and beautiful you will literally be stunned when you see them up close. He uses tried and true reeds to make his calls produce natural and clear sounds. Mark also makes very comfortable call lanyards, customized to your needs. You will not be disappointed with his products.

E.L.K, Inc. (www.elkinc.com)
E.L.K. makes a howler called the Power Howler which has been utilized in one form or another by nearly every caller I know. This howler produces some of the loudest and most realistic howls you'll ever hear. It's a little bulky, and there's a bit of a learning curve, but once you get it down, you'll be howling up dogs in no time.

Edge by Expedite (www.edgebyexpedite.com)
I began using Edge products when I first purchased their Quiver Critter decoy a few years ago. Since then, a lot of animals have died while staring at that decoy! Their staff and customer service is a real breath of fresh air these days – you can email them and they'll actually email you back! They have an entire line of calls and decoys, made for the budget minded hunter, that will help you to bring in that wary animal. If you check their 2009 catalog, you might find a certain someone holding up a bobcat in the 'Predator' pages.

FoxPro (www.gofoxpro.com)
Without a doubt FoxPro is the most popular e-caller on the market. Their callers are high quality, user friendly products that are loaded with features, and their sound library contains the most realistic sounds I've heard yet. They are a little higher priced than some other e-callers, but their customer service includes live people who answer the phone!

GameTraks (www.gametraks.com)
A relatively new player to the e-caller market, GameTraks offers a caller that has great sound quality by using dual directional speakers. It has a very easy to use remote, and has the ability to control up to 6 speakers in the field with one remote, providing the user with the ability to produce "moving" sounds. They also have some of the best battery power in the industry.

Predator Sniper Styx (www.predatorsniperstyx.com)
Maker of the most versatile line of shooting sticks I have ever seen. They also produce the Feather Dancer, a great decoy that is simple to use, easy to carry and deploy, and battery free.

Tru-Spec (www.truspec.com)
I have found that military grade camo holds up better than any other camo I have tried, and their patterns are just as effective as any other commercial line you're going to find. I prefer the

MARPAT camo, but I have seen great results with Multicam and the Desert Digital patterns as well.

Keen (www.keenfootwear.com)
I have tried a number of different hiking boots, both cheap and expensive, but never have I found a boot that fit my foot as well, and was as comfortable as, my Keen boots. They are not joking when they say waterproof, and the boots have a great ability to breath in order to keep your feet dry when you're sweating. The only caution I would give is that a lot of their footwear comes with reflective thread in the laces – you'll want to pull that out before you head to the field for hunting.

Leatherman (www.leatherman.com)
Seriously, do I even need to say anything here? If you don't have one, buy one. Carry it, use it, love it. And their customer service is as trustworthy as their tools.

CamelBak (www.camelbak.com)
Hydration is essential when you're in the outdoors, especially here in Arizona, and I like the convenience of a backpack water supply - it's comfortable and easy to use. CamelBak makes the best hydration bladders out there; I've tried the others. With microbial protection and a host of accessories, you can find a CamelBak that'll work for you.

Rock River Arms (www.rockriverarms.com)
Maker of fine AR-15s, 1911 pistols, and accessories – their AR upper assemblies are hard to beat.

Bushmaster (www.bushmaster.com)
One of the original AR-15 rifle producers, they also make great AR pistols, and I have had nothing but good experiences with their products. Check out their DCM 2-stage trigger - it's fully adjustable has a nice crisp break.

Remington Arms (www.remington.com)
Even Remington makes AR-15s now! They have a great line-up of shotguns – my personal favorite is the 870 series. And their Model 700 rifles are the best bolt guns on the market.

Smith & Wesson (www.smith-wesson.com)
If you don't have an S&W revolver in your safe, you should go out and buy one. And not to be left out of the black rifle market, S&W also makes some fantastic AR-15s in their M&P line.

Bushnell (www.bushnell.com)
A lot of people think Bushnell just makes cheap optics, but they're sadly mistaken. The Trophy and Elite lines are fantastic, and are cost effective, as well. I have used Bushnell products for years, and haven't had one fail me yet.

Remember to take a kid hunting!

About The Author

Glen lives in the high deserts of Arizona with his wonderful wife and three amazing children. He and his family spend every moment they can in the outdoors, whether camping, hiking, hunting, or just enjoying a long evening drive.

Please email Glen or visit his online blog to discuss predator hunting, provide feedback on this book, or to order additional copies:

rizzoisready@gmail.com

rizzoisready.blogspot.com

A few different forum and discussion-based websites were mentioned in this book. You can find Glen on these websites under the following screen names:

PredatorMasters.com	User ID: rizzo
PredatorProfessionals.com	User ID: rizzo (displayed as Glen)
AR15.com	User ID: rizzo1318

Made in the USA
Lexington, KY
27 December 2011